C O N T E N T S

SAFETY FIRST

Though all the designs and methods in this book have been tested for safety, it is not possible to overstate the importance of using the safest construction methods possible. What follows are reminders; some do's and don'ts of basic carpentry. They are not substitutes for your own common sense.

- *Always* use caution, care, and good judgment when following the procedures described in this book.

- *Always* be sure that the electrical setup is safe; be sure that no circuit is overloaded, and that all power tools and electrical outlets are properly grounded. Do not use power tools in wet locations.

- *Always* read container labels on paints, solvents, and other products; provide ventilation, and observe all other warnings.

- *Always* read the tool manufacturer's instructions for using a tool, especially the warnings.

- *Always* use holders or pushers to work pieces shorter than 3 inches on a table saw or jointer. Avoid working short pieces if you can.

- *Always* remove the key from any drill chuck (portable or press) before starting the drill.

- *Always* pay deliberate attention to how a tool works so that you can avoid being injured.

- *Always* know the limitations of your tools. Do not try to force them to do what they were not designed to do.

- *Always* make sure that any adjustment is locked before proceeding. For example, always check the rip fence on a table saw or the bevel adjustment on a portable saw before starting to work.

- *Always* clamp small pieces firmly to a bench or other work surfaces when sawing or drilling.

- *Always* wear the appropriate rubber or work gloves when handling chemicals, heavy construction or when sanding.

- *Always* wear a disposable mask when working with odors, dusts or mists. Use a special respirator when working with toxic substances.

- *Always* wear eye protection, especially when using power tools or striking metal on metal or concrete; a chip can fly off, for example, when chiseling concrete.

- *Always* be aware that there is never time for your body's reflexes to save you from injury from a power tool in a dangerous situation; everything happens too fast. Be *alert!*

- *Always* keep your hands away from the business ends of blades, cutters and bits.

- *Always* hold a portable circular saw with both hands so that you will know where your hands are.

- *Always* use a drill with an auxiliary handle to control the torque when large size bits are used.

- *Always* check your local building codes when planning new construction. The codes are intended to protect public safety and should be observed to the letter.

- *Never* work with power tools when you are tired or under the influence of alcohol or drugs.

- *Never* cut very small pieces of wood or pipe. Whenever possible, cut small pieces off larger pieces.

- *Never* change a blade or a bit unless the power cord is unplugged. Do not depend on the switch being off; you might accidentally hit it.

- *Never* work in insufficient lighting.

- *Never* work while wearing loose clothing, hanging hair, open cuffs, or jewelry.

- *Never* work with dull tools. Have them sharpened, or learn how to sharpen them yourself.

- *Never* use a power tool on a workpiece that is not firmly supported or clamped.

- *Never* saw a workpiece that spans a large distance between horses without close support on either side of the kerf; the piece can bend, closing the kerf and jamming the blade, causing saw kickback.

- *Never* support a workpiece with your leg or other part of your body when sawing.

- *Never* carry sharp or pointed tools, such as utility knives, awls, or chisels in your pocket. If you want to carry tools, use a special-purpose tool belt with leather pockets and holders.

Quick Guide

ROOFING

CREATIVE HOMEOWNER PRESS®

COPYRIGHT © 1995
CREATIVE HOMEOWNER PRESS®
A Division of Federal Marketing Corp.
Upper Saddle River, NJ

Quick Guide is a registered trademark of Creative Homeowner Press®

Manufactured in the United States of America

Editorial Director: David Schiff
Author: David Toht, Greenleaf Publishing, Inc.
Copy Editor: Kimberly Catanzarite
Editorial Assistant: Patrick Quinn
Art Director: Annie Jeon
Graphic Designer: Karen Ellis Phillips
Illustrators: Jim Randolph, Paul M. Schumm
Cover Illustrations: Brian Demeduk
                    Paul M. Schumm

Electronic Prepress: TBC Color Imaging, Inc.
Printed at: Quebecor Printing Inc.

Current Printing (last digit)
10 9 8 7 6 5 4 3 2

Quick Guide: Roofing
LC: 94-071874
ISBN: 1-880029-37-5 (paper)

CREATIVE HOMEOWNER PRESS®
A Division of Federal Marketing Corp.
24 Park Way
Upper Saddle River, NJ 07458

ROOFING TOOLS & MATERIALS

A solid roof is the first line of defense against the elements—few remodeling projects do as much to protect your home. Not only will this job dramatically change the appearance of your home, you will take pride in knowing the job has been done right.

Tools

Many of the tools needed for a roofing job are common to most households. There are some, however, that you probably need to pick up or rent. This chapter discusses the essential tools and equipment necessary for roofing and the wide variety of materials available.

Backsaw

Circular Saw

Crowbar

Hand Saw

Nail Apron

Sliding T-Bevel

Carpenter's Level

Keyhole Saw

Pop Riveter

Chalkline

Tape Measure

Saber Saw

Angle Square

Power Drill

Caulk Gun

Tin Snips

Prybar

Scribing Compass

Utility Knife

Drill Bit Set

Roof Rollers

Roofing Hammer

Framing Square

Claw Hammer

Flat Spade

Working Up High

Working high above the ground is inevitable when repairing or replacing roofing and siding. Common sense, appropriate tools, and a few precautions gets you through the job safely.

Choosing a Ladder

Use a ladder rated Type I (heavy duty, capable of bearing 250 pounds per rung). Wooden ladders are less likely to slide on a gutter or be blown over and they do not conduct electricity. However, they are heavy and difficult to move without assistance. Aluminum ladders are easy to move, but they conduct electricity and may be blown down or knocked over. Expensive fiberglass ladders are relatively light and nonconductive. Make sure your ladder is at least 15 inches wide with rungs that are 12 inches apart. The best of them have nonskid feet and rope-and-pulley extension mechanisms. For eaves, gutter and fascia work, consider padded safety-wall grips.

Ladder Safety

Working on a ladder is inherently dangerous. Perhaps the biggest danger is becoming too comfortable. It's easy to become cavalier and try to reach just a little bit further to paint a spot without moving the ladder. Don't do it. Here are some other important things to consider when working on a ladder.

Getting the Correct Angle. The angle at which the ladder leans against the house is very important. If the angle is too great, the ladder is subject to strain and may break or bend. If the angle is too small, the ladder is likely to fall backward. Position the ladder so that the feet are at least one foot from the house for every four feet that the ladder is extended.

Leveling the Ladder. If the ground is so soft that a leg of the ladder might sink and cause it to tip to one side, set the ladder on a piece of plywood.

Leveling the Ladder. Make sure the feet of the ladder stand on a level surface. If necessary, shim the legs.

Choosing a Ladder. Ladders must be at least 15 in. wide with 12 in. between rungs.

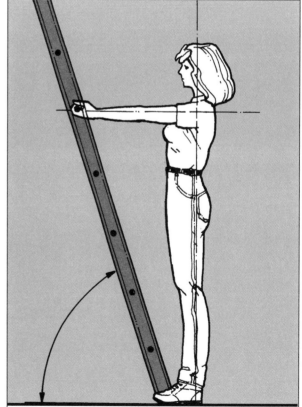

Getting the Correct Angle. Firemen use this quick method for determining the correct angle for leaning a ladder.

Extending the Ladder. Be sure the ladder extends 3 feet above the edge of the roof to permit a firm grip as you step onto the roof. Climb onto a roof from the eaves side only—never over a gable. Move the ladder frequently rather than trying to reach by leaning.

Climbing & Carrying

Always face forward and keep your hips within the rails of the ladder. Allow only one person on the ladder at a time. Bundles of shingles or rolls of roofing are best carried on one shoulder and steadied by one hand. Be wary of loose material on roofs, particularly wet leaves, loose granules and detached shingles. Do not climb inclined roofs unless they are thoroughly dry. As a precaution, thoroughly sweep the area where you are working and wear shoes with rubber soles.

Caution: *Always be aware of the location of electrical lines, particularly when moving a ladder. An aluminum or wet wooden ladder is conductive and can transmit a fatal shock.*

Choosing Cleats & Brackets

Adequate scaffolding and working platforms make a roofing or siding job easier and safer and can be rented for the duration of a job. They range from simple metal cleats to movable pump jacks that are raised or lowered as necessary.

Metal Cleats. Held by 16d nails hammered into the rafters where possible, metal cleats are placed beneath shingle tabs so nailholes can be sealed later. The cleats are installed at 6-foot intervals and hold a length of 2x4 that provides a working ledge. To remove the cleats, pull them out or firmly hammer the nail. Then coat the underside of the tab with roofing cement and press firmly.

Ladder Jacks. Consider using ladder jacks for working under eaves or when applying siding. They are attached to the top of the ladder or slung underneath, and can support a 2x10 work platform up to 9 feet long.

Metal Cleats. Anchored with 16d nails, cleats hold a length of 2x4, creating a handy foothold.

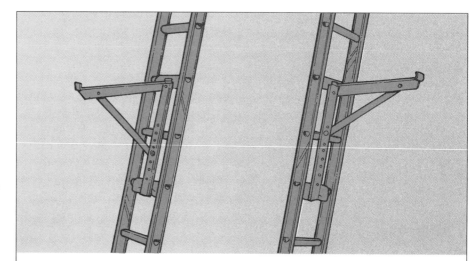

Ladder Jacks. Ideal for work under eaves and for laying the starter course of roofing, ladder jacks adjust with relative ease.

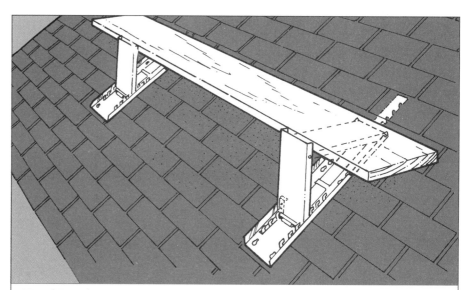

Roof Brackets. With a plank set flat, roof brackets offer more room for tools and materials than metal cleats do.

Roof Brackets. Available in many forms, roof brackets attach to 16d nails that are hammered under shingles and hold a plank working platform that can be moved as the job progresses.

Pump Jacks. These movable platform supports are raised and lowered to suit the task. When you pump the lever with your foot they ride up and down a pair of doubled 2x4s. You can add accessory brackets to make a handy elevated workbench. Pump jacks also operate as freight elevators for raising large or heavy objects.

Pump Jacks. This affordable type of scaffolding rides on doubled 2x4s set vertically.

Roofing Materials

Composition Shingles

Composition shingles are relatively simple to apply, last 15 to 20 years, and come in a wide variety of colors, profiles and textures. These shingles, which are by far the most common roofing material in North America, are made with felt, wood fiber, or most typically these days, fiberglass mat impregnated with asphalt and coated with mineral granules. Most shingles have adhesive beneath the tabs to keep them from curling or blowing back. They are flexible and therefore adaptable, and can wrap almost all roof shapes and contours. They also suit every climate in North America.

Shingles can be applied to any roof that has a pitch of 4 in 12 (four inches rise for every 12 inches of run) or more. With double felt underlayment, they can be applied to a roof with a pitch as low as 2 in 12 if shingle tabs are sealed down.

Often composition shingles are applied over an old roof of the same type. Three layers can be built up before all must be torn off (more than three layers are permissible only if the framing can bear the weight, and nails must be long enough to penetrate at least 3/4 inch into the decking). If a tear-off is required, repair sheathing and remove all loose or protruding nails. Staples are used on new roofs and on roofs that have been stripped of old roofing.

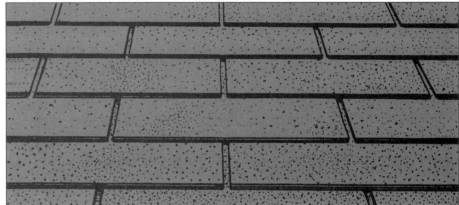

Composition Shingles. By far the most common roofing material in North America, composition shingles are relatively simple to apply, last 15 to 20 years, and are available in a wide variety of colors, profiles and textures.

Types of Shingles

There are many styles of composition shingles. You can purchase them with three tabs that suggest three slate or wooden shingles, with two tabs, or strip shingles with no tabs. Also available are multi-layered textured shingles designed to look like wood shakes.

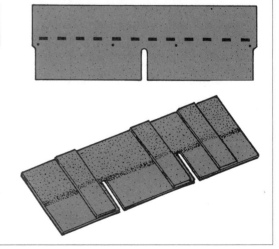

Roll Roofing

Ideal for porches with shallow slopes, garages and utility buildings, roll roofing is quick and easy to apply. It is the least expensive option for roofs that have a very slight pitch. Roll roofing is not as attractive as composite shingles, but roofs with very shallow pitches are not visible from the ground anyway. One type of roll roofing, sometimes called selvage, is designed to be applied with a half-lap to provide double coverage. Selvage can be used with pitches as low as 1 in 12 (1 inch rise per 12 inches of run). Roll roofing is 36 inches wide and is available in a variety of colors. It can be applied with nails revealed (on slopes of 2 in 12 or more) or with nails covered by the roofing (on more shallow slopes).

Wood Shingles & Shakes

Among the most beautiful roofing materials are red cedar shingles and shakes. They have twice the insulation value of asphalt shingles, are lighter in weight than most other roofing materials, and are very resistant to hail damage. They also are well-suited to withstand the freeze-thaw conditions of variable climates. Wood shingles are machine cut and smoothed on both sides, while shakes are thicker and rough on at least one side. Pressure-injected fire retardant, as indicated by the indus-

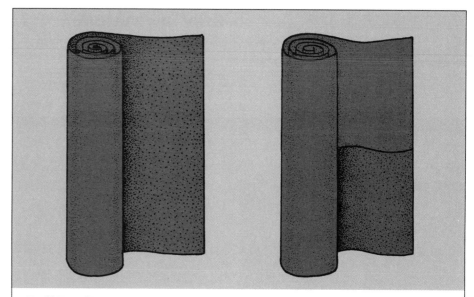

Roll Roofing. Roll roofing is 36 inches wide and comes in two types. One type has mineral granules covering the entire face and is applied with courses overlapping only 2 inches. The other type, sometimes called selvage, has granules on only half its face. Roofing cement or hot asphalt is applied to the non-granule side which is then covered with the next course of roofing. This double coverage roofing is for very slight pitches.

try designation "Certi-Guard," conforms to all state and local building codes for use in fire hazard regions. Given periodic coatings of wood preservative, shingles and shakes serve for 50 years or more. The drawbacks of using them include their high cost and slow application time.

Shakes differ from wood shingles in that they are split on one face and machine smoothed on the other. They vary in thickness and have a rustic,

varied appearance. Because the rough surface of the split face sometimes allows water back under the shakes, a layer of underlayment (asphalt-saturated felt or fiberglass) is used between each course.

Both shingles and shakes require 1x4 sheathing spaced to suit the desired exposure. Along the roof rake and roof eaves 1x6 sheathing supports underlayment and seals the roof.

Wood Shingles and Shakes. Although quite simple, the installation of wood shingles and shakes is a time-consuming job.

Wood Fiber Shingle Panels. A relatively new product, these panels install quickly and weather to a shingle-like gray.

Slate. One of the oldest roofing materials, slate is beautiful, long lasting and very expensive.

Wood Fiber Shingle Panels.
Another wood shingle option that is suitable for roofs with a 4 in 12 pitch is hardboard shingle panels. With scored nailing and alignment lines to ease application, these shingles are installed in half the time it takes to apply cedar shakes. The panels do not crack with age and weather to a light gray. Shingle panels are 12x48 inches.

Slate

Fireproof and extremely durable as well as beautiful, slate is among the oldest roofing material. Today it is also among the most expensive. In addition it requires special framing (designed to bear a heavier weight) and special furring. Difficult to cut and apply, slate roofing is definitely a job left to the professionals.

Synthetic Slate. Made of cement-impregnated non-asbestos fiber, synthetic slate looks like the real thing but weighs a lot less. Synthetic slate does not contain combustible materials and therefore carries the highest fire rating (Class A) from Underwriters' Laboratories. Some brands carry a warranty of 40 years. Synthetic slate is an expensive material. It typically is used on homes where historically appropriate

Synthetic Slate. Cement-impregnated fiber creates a long-lasting imitation of the real thing.

materials are required. The material is difficult to cut and must be nailed carefully to avoid cracking the shingles. This is another job for experienced professionals.

Built-Up Roofing

Built-up roofing is suitable only for flat roofs and roofs with very slight pitches. For this reason it is used on many contemporary, flat-roofed homes and on slightly pitched porch roofs. Because it requires hot asphalt,

a contractor must handle this job and the roof must have a minimum slope of 1/4 inch per foot (no roof can have a slope of less than this anyway).

The oldest type of built-up roofing consists of several alternating layers of hot asphalt and felt. The final layer of asphalt is topped with pea gravel.

An increasingly common form of built-up roofing employs a large sheet of modified bitumen membrane to improve protection for flat or slightly sloped roofs. There are two types: plasticized (also called atacitic polypropylene (APP), and rubberized (also called (styrene-butadiene-styrene (SBS)). These relatively new materials are less prone to damage caused by ultraviolet rays. They have a higher melting point and therefore are slower to soften in direct sunlight. They also are more stable than roll roofing or felt . Since the application of plasticized roofing involves heating the bottom of the material with a propane torch, a contractor is required for the job. Granules or foil are added as a final layer for ultraviolet protection.

One advantage to using rubberized roofing is its ability to stretch in extreme temperatures. It may be heat welded, or applied with hot asphalt or a cold adhesive. Both rubberized and plasticized roofing benefit from a layer of fiberglass membrane for additional strength.

Metal Roofing

Widely used on commercial buildings, metal roofing is increasingly marketed for residential use. Depending on slope and framing, metal roofing can be installed over old roofing. It costs as much as three times more than conventional roofing but can last from 20 to 50 years with almost no maintenance. Unlike the old galvanized tin roofs, metal roofing today is made of steel with an alloy coating of aluminum and zinc. A wide spectrum of colors are available.

Many different profiles are available but the simple standing seam style (overlapping ridges run parallel to the eaves) is the most appropriate for older homes that might have had a tin roof at one time. This material usually requires professional application, and while the popularity of metal roofing is quickly increasing, a network of qualified residential contractors is only slowly developing.

Ceramic Tile

Ceramic tile roofs, often used in the West, Southwest, and parts of the South, can last as long as the house itself. New fiber-reinforced concrete products are less costly, easier to install, more uniform in appearance, and have most of the attributes of ceramic tile. Beyond replacing cracked or missing tiles, the do-it-yourselfer probably will want to hire a professional for this difficult job.

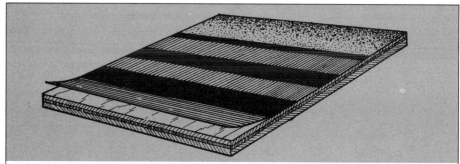

Built-Up Roofing. This material derives its name from the layers that combine to create a water-resistant surface. Pea gravel protects the roof from ultraviolet rays.

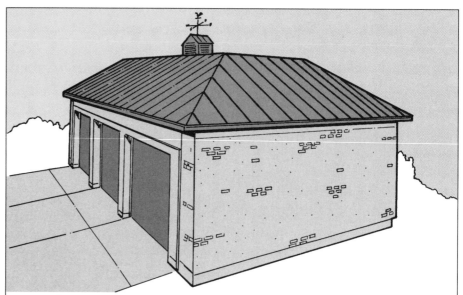

Metal Roofing. Metal roofing is making a comeback. With minimal maintenance it lasts up to 50 years.

Ceramic Tile. Ceramic tile roofs require special framing and expert installation. Repairs are within the skill of the do-it-yourselfer, but whole roof installation is still left to the professionals.

REPAIRING ROOFING

Do not panic if you find a leak in the roof. One leak does not necessarily mean the entire roof needs to be replaced. A bit of detective work often points to a damaged area that can be repaired. This chapter demonstrates how to trace and repair such a leak.

Tracing Roof Leaks

The best way to detect a leak is to locate dampness or a trail of discoloration in the attic. Do not, however, expect the leak to be directly above a damp ceiling or wall. Most likely the leaking water has traveled beneath the roofing material and down a rafter or truss member before appearing on the interior ceiling or wall.

The best way to find a leak is to examine the underside of the roof from the attic. If your attic does not have a floor be careful to step only on the floor joists (never step on the insulation between the joists). Better yet, set boards or a piece of 1/2-inch plywood perpendicular to the joists. Make sure the ends of the lumber extend far enough past each joist to prevent tipping.

With a powerful light source inspect the undersides of the sheathing in the general area where the stain has appeared. Sheathing is usually made up of plywood but yours may be made of shiplap planks. In the case of very old houses, you may find no roof sheathing, only lath nailed across the rafters with wooden or slate shingles nailed on top of the lath. Good sheathing or lath is uniformly aged and completely dry even after a rain. Check for dampness and discoloration and pay special attention to the places where the roof is penetrated by the chimney, air vent or plumbing vent pipes. If sheathing is dark, damp or crumbling, check for wood rot by probing with a screwdriver. Rotten wood must be replaced.

Water always runs in a downward direction so once you find dampness search for the source of the water's path above the moisture. Water may pool on flat surfaces, but it always finds its way downward even if it runs along what appears to be a horizontal surface.

When the leak is discovered mark the area to be repaired. If you are going to make the repair immediately, pierce through the sheathing from underneath with a nail, extended drill bit or awl. If not, measure from the attic wall framing and ridge or eaves. Allow for the thickness of the wall and the outward extension of the eaves when taking measurements.

Making Emergency Roof Repairs

Damage from fallen tree limbs, violent storms and exceptional snow build-up is an unwelcome surprise. Here are some interior and exterior solutions to leaks.

Limiting the Damage. Limit the water damage as quickly as possible by placing a bucket as close to the leak as possible. Remove and discard soaked attic insulation. A string attached to the leak guides the water to the bucket.

Providing Protection. Cover large areas of damage with a fiber-reinforced plastic dropcloth. Place boards under the dropcloth to create a high spot that will carry water away from the damaged area.

Fixing a Shingle. To fix a broken or missing shingle in an emergency situation slip a piece of scrap sheet metal or aluminum flashing under the damaged shingle. Tap it with a block of wood to force it under the course above.

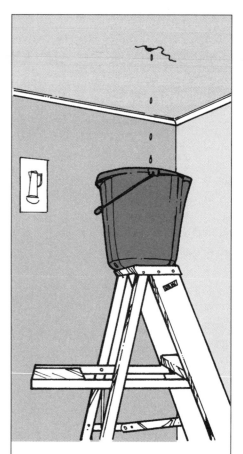

Limiting the Damage. Catch the water as soon as possible, mop up and remove any soaked materials.

Fixing a Shingle. A simple piece of metal shoved under a shingle tab holds until a more permanent patch is made.

Providing Protection. Cover the leak if possible to prevent additional damage.

Locating Trouble Spots

If your roof has a leak check the trouble spots to determine where the leak originates. Trouble spots are those places well known for causing leaks. They include valleys, flashing along walls and around objects that penetrate the roof (such as chimneys, air vents and plumbing stacks), rotting doors, gutters, eaves encrusted with ice and popped nails. Keep in mind that almost all flat roofs eventually experience problems.

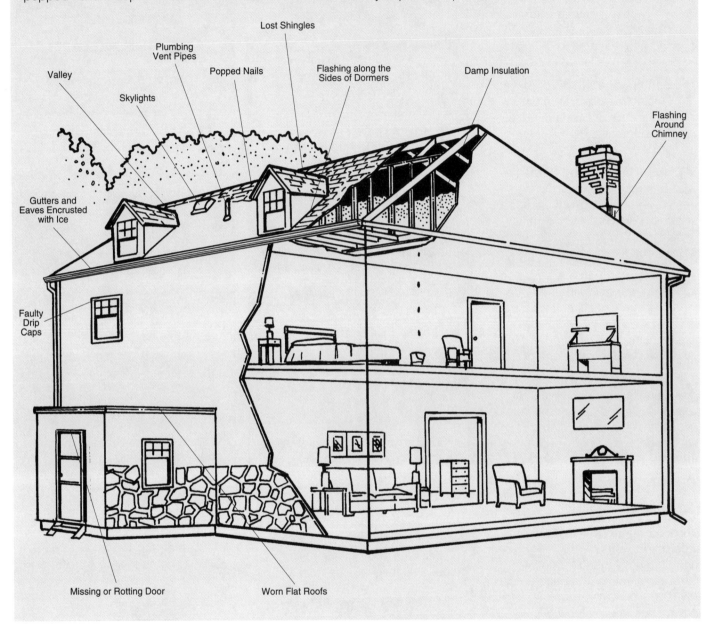

Lost Shingles

Plumbing
Vent Pipes

Valley

Popped Nails

Skylights

Flashing along the
Sides of Dormers

Damp Insulation

Flashing
Around
Chimney

Gutters and
Eaves Encrusted
with Ice

Faulty
Drip
Caps

Missing or Rotting Door

Worn Flat Roofs

Making Temporary Roof Repairs

Equipped with hammer, pry bar, galvanized roofing nails, roofing cement and spare shingles, a do-it-yourselfer can quickly make repairs to protect the home temporarily. When dealing with shingles remember to tuck the topmost edge of new shingles or patches beneath the course above. This overlap sheds water in a downward direction.

To temporarily repair wind-torn shingles, glue down both sides of the tear with roofing cement. Nail both sides and apply cement over the heads of the nails. Applying a small amount of cement to the shank of the nail before hammering it home creates an especially good seal. In a similar fashion, curled shingles are glued down with roofing cement. This is best done on a hot day when the shingles are warm and supple. Nail them if necessary, coating the nail shanks and heads with roofing cement.

Repairing Blisters on Built-Up Roofs

With time, blisters may appear on built-up roofs. This occurs because moisture that is trapped under one of the layers of the roof expands due to extreme heat and causes bubbles to form. The bubbles must be lanced, flattened and resealed to eliminate the possibility of a future leak.

1 Splitting the Blister. Begin by lancing the blister with a utility knife. Take care not to damage the layers underneath. Allow moisture beneath the blister to dry.

2 Applying Roofing Cement. Before flattening, apply a generous layer of roofing cement into the blistered area. Be sure to work the cement well under the interior edges. Nail the patch in place.

3 Applying a Patch. Use a piece of 90-pound roofing paper to cut out a patch that is at least 3 inches larger than the blistered area in all directions. Nail it and cover the entire area with roofing cement

4 Re-applying Gravel. If weather permits let the patch dry for several days. Then pour roofing tar (not cement) onto the patch and evenly sprinkle pea gravel over the patch so that it matches the rest of the roof.

Patching Flat Roofs

Worn roofing, popped nails and separated seams are the most common problems. Standing water on low spots often forces leakage. One advantage of having a leak on a flat roof is that it is easier to work on than an angled roof. A disadvantage is that water can find any gaps left in the patch and the patch itself can act as a dam, eventually creating another leak-prone pool. Follow these steps carefully, filling all gaps while keeping the profile of the patch as smooth as possible.

1 Cutting away Damaged Roofing. A tear or crack is repaired by cutting a rectangular

1 Cut the blister open with a utility knife without damaging the layers underneath.

2 Push roofing cement under the edges of the blister.

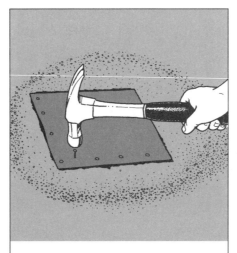

3 Cut a patch larger than the damaged area and nail every two inches around the perimeter.

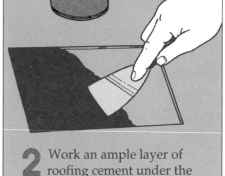

4 After letting the patch dry, coat the area with roofing tar and cover it with pea gravel.

patch. You can use a piece of composite shingle or roll roofing for the patch. Cut the patch larger than the area of the crack and use it as a guide for cutting into the roofing

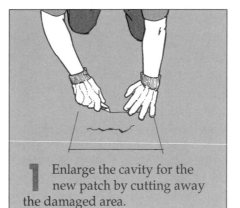

1 Enlarge the cavity for the new patch by cutting away the damaged area.

material. Cut into the old roofing and remove the damaged area.

2 Cementing the Patch. Use a putty knife to smooth roofing cement into the area you have cut

2 Work an ample layer of roofing cement under the edges of the cavity.

out. Be sure to work cement well under the cut edges. If there is more than one layer of roofing, add layers of cement and equal size patches until the surface of the patch is even with the surface of the roof.

3 **Nailing and Applying Cement.** Nail around the edges of the patch and apply another layer of cement. This time overlap the joint of the patch by at least 2 inches.

4 **Adding a Final Cover.** Add a final cover of roofing material, once again overlapping the patch area by at least 2 inches. Press down firmly but do not nail. If nails have popped out nail them down and coat the heads with roofing cement.

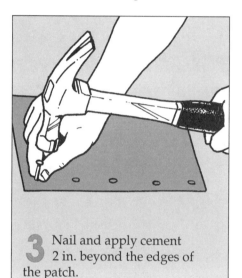

3 Nail and apply cement 2 in. beyond the edges of the patch.

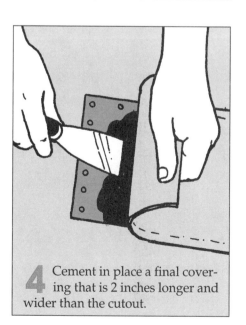

4 Cement in place a final covering that is 2 inches longer and wider than the cutout.

Making Permanent Shingle Repairs

If the roof is sound except for some isolated shingle damage, there is a way to repair composition shingles. To make your working area as safe and convenient as possible while making these repairs, note the information on ladders and roof brackets (see pages 7-9).

1 **Removing Nails.** Each shingle is held in place by two sets of four nails: one set directly pierces the shingle and the other pierces the shingle after passing through the course above. Remove the damaged shingle by first pulling out the nails that pass through the shingle above into the damaged shingle. Then pull out the nails that pass directly through the damaged shingle. To get at the nails, hold the tabs back and use a flat prybar to pry out the nails. You may need to release the adhesive seals by levering underneath with the prybar, but be careful not to crack the shingle when working in cooler weather.

2 **Replacing the Shingle.** Slip a new shingle in place, aligning it with the tabs on either side. If the weather is warm enough to make the tabs supple simply bend them up and nail the shingle in place with galvanized roofing nails.

If you are making the repair in cool weather you may want to use the flat end of a crowbar or prybar to hammer the nail. Hammer on the bar as near as possible to the nailhead without hitting the shingles.

3 **Sealing the Shingle.** Place a small amount of roofing cement under the tabs and press down. This holds shingles down until they settle into place with warm weather.

1 Use a prybar to pry out nails in the the damaged shingle and in the course above.

2 Slip a new shingle into place aligned with the tabs on either side.

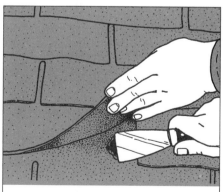

3 Use roofing cement to hold down the tabs that were bent back.

Repairing Wood Shingles & Shakes

1 Splitting and Removing the Shingle. Replacing wood shingles and shakes can be complicated because shingles and shakes are not flexible and crack relatively easily. If a shingle is badly rotted or cracked remove it by splitting it with a chisel or the sharp end of a prybar. Pull out the pieces carefully without damaging the 24-inch strip of heavy-duty roofing felt (called underlayment) that lays beneath each course of shingles.

2 Cutting Nails. Use a hacksaw blade (wrap electrical tape around one end to spare your fingers) to cut the nails that remain under the shingle that overlaps the area. Cut them as flush to the shingle.

3 Cutting a Replacement Shingle or Shake. Use the hatchet end of a roofing hammer to split a shingle or shake to size. Use a utility knife or block plane to fine tune the width so for a 1/8- to 1/4-inch gap on both sides of the replacement shingle.

4 Installing the New Shingle. Slip the shingle into place. Then tap it with a block of wood and a hammer until it is within 1 inch of the course line. Toenail it in place, driving two 4d galvanized nails just at the course edge. Use a nail set to drive the nails home without damaging the shingle above.

5 Forcing the Shingle into Place. Use a block to hammer the shingle under the course. As you do so, the nailheads move under the overlapping course sealing them tightly.

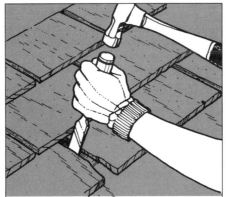

1 Remove the damaged shingle by splitting it in several places with a wood chisel.

2 With a hacksaw blade cut off the nails under the course above. Cut nails flush to the shingle.

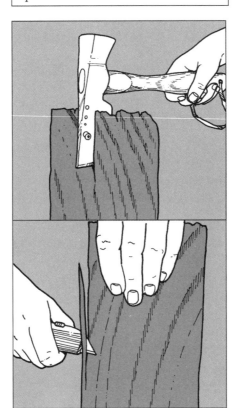

3 Split the shingle to size (top). Shave the shingle to the exact width (bottom).

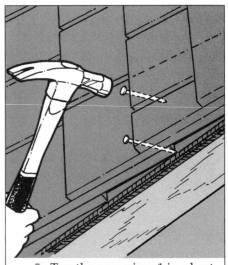

4 Tap the new piece 1 in. short of the course line. Toenail with two 8d galvanized nails.

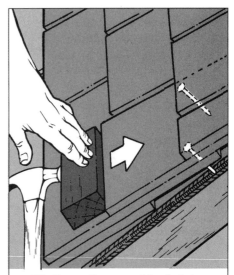

5 Force the new shingle into place by hammering the piece of scrap.

Repairing a Ridge Shingle

A crack in the ridge (usually caused by a fallen tree limb) is repaired by cutting a shingle tab to size and cementing it in place. Bend the patch gently to match the curve of the ridge and slip one edge of it under the lip of the ridge shingle nearest the damage.

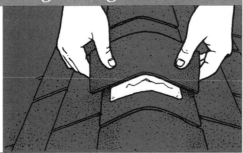

Repairing & Replacing Flashing

Flashing is the crucial water barrier between the roof and vertical surfaces such as chimneys, vents and walls. It is made of sheet metal or roll roofing. Flashing fails when it rusts, becomes punctured or loosens. Complete flashing replacement is best done after removing a roof or before a new layer of roofing is installed. Roofing cement works wonders for breakdown maintenance until thorough repairs can be made.

Flashing leaks often are the result of bent or loose metal flashing, or worn or punctured roll roofing. Simply bend pieces of metal flashing to their original shape, then renail and caulk with asphalt. Flashing that is fitted into mortar joints on chimneys sometimes loosens. In this case chip out the loose mortar and replace with mortar or latex mortar caulk.

Repairing Fascia & Eaves Damage

If the eaves are in disrepair weather and small animals may invade the roof. An ideal time for eaves replacement is before adding a new roof or a new layer of roofing. Eaves damage typically is caused by faulty gutters and deteriorated roofing. Eaves repairs require a good working platform (scaffolding is ideal) and an assistant.

1 **Removing the Gutter.** To rebuild a section of eaves, remove the overlapping run of gutter. First detach the gutter from the downspout by removing the sheet metal screws. Both ends of the gutter must be supported until lowered to the ground.

2 **Removing Damaged Wood.** Pry off the damaged fascia from the rafter ends. If a complete fascia board is not removed, make a cut over the middle of a rafter end.

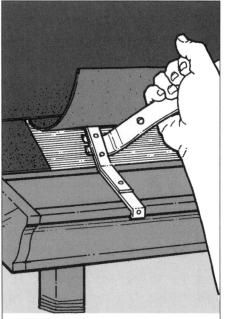

1 Pull back a shingle tab to reveal the nails holding the strap of the gutter hanger.

Choose a location for the cut and pull the nails out with a "cat's paw" nail remover. Then mark the cutting line and make the cut with a hand saw. Sometimes the end of the rafter may be too chewed up to provide good nailing when replacing the board. If this is the case add a sister (a small nailing block nailed to the side of the rafter) flush to the end.

3 **Replacing Eaves Fascia.** Cut new boards to length and prime on both sides. With the help of an assistant nail the board in place. (If you are working alone, this old carpenter's trick helps: Hammer a nail into the top edge of the new fascia, then bend it over and use it as a hook to hold one end in place while you nail the other end.)

2 Pry off damaged fascia. To remove a section cut over a rafter.

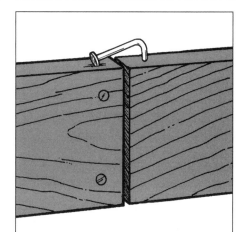

3 Use a bent nail in the top of the fascia to hook one end in place while you nail the other end. Attach the new fascia with two 8d galvanized nails into each rafter. Toenail slightly at joints.

Repairing Cracks & Splits

Minor cracks (up to 1/2 inch) are patched with roofing cement. For a larger cracks, apply a couple of dabs of roofing cement to the underside of a piece of sheet aluminum and slip it under the shingle. Bowed shingles or shakes are remedied by splitting the bowed shingles lengthwise with a chisel. Remove about 1/4 inch of the shingle at the split so it lays down flat. Drill pilot holes and nail either side of the split. Finish the job by applying a coat of roofing cement over the split.

4 Straightening New Wood.
Rafter ends are seldom even. Hammer two 8d galvanized nails (one above the other) where the fascia touches a rafter end. Stretch a cord or chalkline from end to end of the fascia. Note where the face of the board cups or bows out. Tap from behind in cupped sections and insert builder's shim between the rafter and the fascia. Prime replacement molding. Then cut and nail in place, overlapping fascia joints for a seamless finish.

5 Replacing Damaged Soffit.
If the fascia is damaged, the soffit is probably damaged as well and will need to be replaced. Sizes and materials vary but the procedure is roughly the same. Remove the damaged area, including trim found beneath the soffit. Be sure that you add the replacement where there is a rafter end for nailing. Cut the replacement piece to size and use the damaged piece as a guide to mark the locations of the rafters on the replacement piece. Tack two 8d nails at each mark (it is easier than trying to start the nails upside down). Tack a nail into the wall of your house to support one end of the soffit as you push it into place.

6 Getting a Tight Fit. Tack the soffit in place but do not drive the nails home. Pry the soffit outward with a prybar until you have a tight joint between the fascia and the soffit. Complete nailing and replace trim if necessary.

4 Set a taut line as a guide for straightening replacement fascia. Hammer outward from under the eaves to correct an inward bow.

5 Soffit damage often occurs where there is fascia damage. After removing the damage, cut a new piece to size. Mark nailing points and start nails before pushing the new soffit into place.

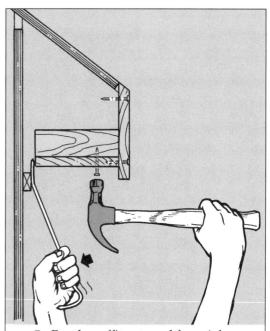

6 Pry the soffit outward for a tight, straight fit with the fascia. Replace any soffit trim previously removed.

PREPARING & FLASHING THE ROOF

Roof decking, underlayment, and flashing are the foundation of a long-lasting roof. Even the best shingling job is undercut by incomplete underlayment and voids or rotten boards in the decking. The many varieties of flashing protect the roof at its most vulnerable points.

Tear-Off or Reroof?

A reroofing job consists of applying new roofing material over the existing surface. This is less expensive and easier than a "tear-off" job which requires that the old roofing be stripped off and hauled away.

Old tile and slate roofs cannot be covered over. Because they are heavy and impossible to nail through, they must be torn off. Roll roofing placed over any other surface (even shingles) is unsightly. If the house can take another layer of roofing, make sure there is a sound foundation for nailing and an even surface for the new shingles.

1 **Counting the Layers.** The first step in determining whether or not you can reroof is to check the rake of the roof to determine how many roofing layers exist. The rake is the sloped edge of the roof. Remember that drip edge sometimes is applied before reroofing and may hide evidence of previous layers. Once the number of layers is determined, check local roofing codes for the maximum number of roofing layers allowed. The answer varies depending on the type of roofing materials and the pitch of the roof. For wood shingles codes typically allow the original roof plus one reroof. For asphalt shingles codes typically allow the original plus two reroofs. Ask your local building inspector for specifics.

2 **Checking for Solid Sheathing.** All rotten boards under the old roofing must be replaced. Go into the attic and examine all suspicious spots including voids and separating plywood. Check for rot by poking with a screwdriver. If the rot is limited to a few places you need only remove the old roofing and replace the boards in those spots. If necessary, build up the roofing above the replacement sheathing with extra layers of shingles to make a flush surface for the new roof.

3 **Checking Surface Conditions.** Do not expect the new roofing to smooth over dips and waves found

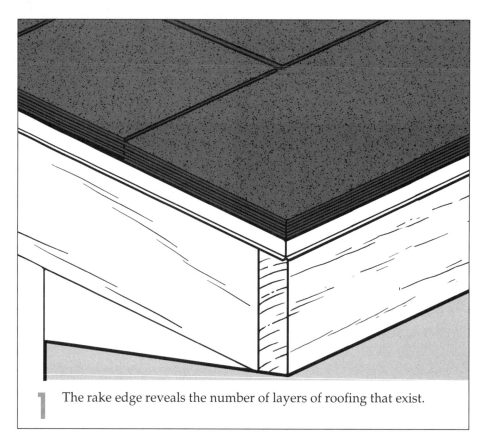

1 The rake edge reveals the number of layers of roofing that exist.

in the old roofing. If the surface of the old roofing is not uniformly flat it must be removed. Shake roofs, shingle roofs which have curled excessively, and old-style interlocking shingles, must be torn off.

Caution: *If you reroof when a tear-off is called for, the results may include costly structural damage to your home and possible fines for violating local codes.*

2 Check between rafters for any signs of deterioration of the sheathing.

3 Make sure old roofing lays flat before adding a new layer of roofing.

Tear-Off Techniques

Removing an old roof is a matter of hard, physical work and although no special skills are required, a bit of planning and preparation makes the job less difficult.

Tearing-off creates a massive amount of debris, so plan ahead by calling several dumpster rental companies to get the best price. If you tell them the square footage of the roof and the number of roofing layers that are to be torn off, they can estimate the size and number of containers needed. Choose the location for the dumpster carefully, minimizing damage to landscaping and limiting carrying distance as much as possible.

Warn your neighbors ahead of time and get their permission if you need to place the dumpster on their property. Place dropcloths wherever debris is likely to fall; nails and broken shingles wreak havoc with the lawn mower. If you are lucky the shingles may come off in large groups (this indicates that they were not nailed down properly). Usually shingles come off two or three at a time.

1 Starting at the Top. Begin at the ridge and work your way down (this is especially important for wood shingles so debris does not fall through the open sheathing). Tear off wood shingles or shakes by sliding a crowbar or prybar underneath and pulling sharply upward. This loosens several rows at a time.

2 Saving Old Flashing. Remove flashing carefully so it can be used as a template for new flashing. If old shingles and nails are removed with care the flashing can be reused. In the case of chimney flashing where the upper part may be embedded in mortar, you may be able to carefully bend the flashing out of the way rather than go through the trouble to remove it.

3 Inspecting the Deck. Once you have removed the old roofing, inspect all of the sheathing and replace broken or rotten pieces with a material of the same thickness. On older homes the sheathing may be 7/8 inch to 1 inch thick. Plywood sheathing is not available in thicknesses greater than 3/4 inch. Use extra layers of felt or roofing materials to make up the difference.

1 Use a crowbar to tear off shingles, working from the ridge downward.

2 If old flashing is in good condition pull it back to allow for the new roof, then reuse it.

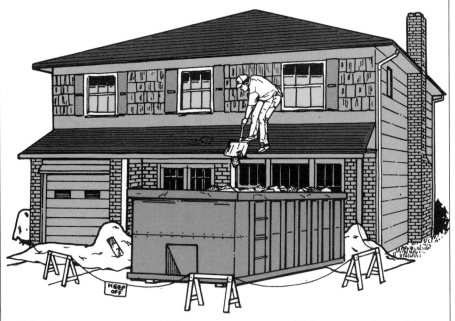

If the dumpster sits in a public access area rope off the area and provide signs in accordance with local ordinances.

3 Replace damaged areas of the decking before reroofing.

Applying Underlayment

1 Rolling out the Felt. Roofs that have been stripped down to the sheathing require a layer of underlayment before flashing and reroofing. Check the instructions on the roofing material that you are using to determine whether you need 15- or 30-pound felt. Be sure the deck is dry before starting the job. There is no need for extensive nailing unless you plan to leave the felt exposed for a few days, or if you are working in windy conditions. The nailing for the shingles will hold the felt permanently in place. Roofing nails are acceptable but 1/4- to 5/16-inch staples are quicker to apply and usually do the trick just as well. A staple hammer (also known as a hammer tacker) speeds up the job. Be sure nails or staples are hammered completely flush.

2 Overlapping Courses. Overlap the felt 2 inches (white lines printed on the felt provide a 2-inch guide). It must be flat and smooth. When working in the hot sun lay only as much as you can cover with roofing in an hour or so as heat causes exposed felt to buckle.

3 Trimming for Stacks and Vents. Underlayment is installed before flashing. Trim it back so that it does not buckle from being too close to the vents or stacks.

Even if the job does not require tearing off the old roofing, there is plenty of serious preparation to take care of before reroofing. The deck must be cleared for the new roof.

■ Ridge shingles are removed with a flat bar or levered off with a flat shovel. Be careful to sweep away all debris—especially loose nails (top left).

■ To ensure a smooth-looking roof nail down curled shingles and fill in spaces where shingles have cracked off (top right).

■ Remove protruding nails or hammer them flush. Sweep well; a loose nail wedged under a shingle is a leak just waiting to happen (bottom left).

■ Remove all exposed old flashing such as the vent stack flashing shown. Exposed metal flashing in the valleys, called open valley flashing, can be left if you are sure it will last 25 more years (bottom right).

1 Unroll the felt and tack the upper corner of the end. Cut to fit after fastening.

2 The felt overlaps 2 in. lengthwise. Allow at least 4 in. in places that overlap on the side.

3 Cut carefully around vent stacks so the felt lays flat and does not create gaps.

Applying Flashing

Flashing is applied in places where regular roofing materials cannot prevent leaks. It is found around vent pipes, chimneys and skylights, and also is used in valleys that connect two sections of roof, in places where the roof meets a side of the house, and on the ends of eaves and rakes. Flashing is made of galvanized sheet metal, aluminum or copper. Roofing cement is used in conjunction with flashing but cement alone can't do the job. If the original flashing did its job well, use it as a guide for applying new pieces. Keep sections of the old flashing for templates and install the new flashing in the same place and manner as the old. If the old flashing leaked and you cannot locate the source of the problem, it is best to call in a professional.

The nails used must be made of the same material as the flashing. A mixture of aluminum, tin, steel or copper may cause corrosion or discoloration.

If you find that the roof suffered from blistering, wore out prematurely, had an exceptional number of buckled shingles, and you find evidence of moisture damage in rafters or attic insulation, it may be an indication that the roof needs additional vents. In the case of roof vents, the rule of thumb is one square foot of ventilating area per 150 square feet of attic space. If you determine that the roof needs additional vents now is the time to install them.

Valley Flashing

Valley flashing is installed on top of the underlayment, but beneath the roofing. The two basic types of valley treatments are called open and closed. If the flashing material is visible after the roof is finished it is considered open. If the roofing material covers the flashing it is considered closed. Open flashing works for all types of roofs. On the other hand, closed flashing is used only for composition shingles. Open valleys are essential for wooden shingles, slate and tile because the nature of materials do not allow them to overlap to make a closed valley. Open valleys also are commonly used with asphalt shingles that have metal or roll roofing flashing. Open valley flashing is the more complicated to apply, but provides greater protection, especially from torrential downpours and the slow melt of heavy snow.

Installing Open Valley Flashing

If you are reroofing a roof that has open flashing be certain that the old flashing will last as long as the new roof. If not, you may have to remove the old flashing by cutting out a section of the old roofing wide enough to allow its removal. Install new flashing and fill in the remaining space with roofing material.

W-Metal. For open valleys it is preferable to use preformed W-metal (so called because in profile it looks somewhat like the letter W). This type of flashing has a ridge bent in the middle to prevent water from rushing down one roof slope and under the shingles on the other slope.

In an open valley the exposed portion of the flashing is wider at the bottom than at the top to allow better drainage. On either side of the valley, snap chalk lines that begin 6 inches apart at the top and widen at the rate of about 1/8 inch per foot as they descend.

Waterproofing Shingle Underlayment

A roof depends on gravity to make water run down and off, but when held back by ice, or during intense driving rain, water can work its way up and under even properly installed shingles. Because normal felt underlayment is not completely waterproof, especially around nail holes, water can work its way in. For those who experience harsh winters, it's reassuring to know you can install additional insurance against water damage.

Waterproof shingle underlayment is a special material made of asphalt and elastic polymers designed to adhere tightly to roof sheathing and around the shanks of nails driven through it. This self-sealing attribute ensures that water cannot get past it, even where you drive a nail.

Install the underlayment along those areas where ice dams and driving rain can create a problem, or where water tends to accumulate: along the eaves, around skylights, in valleys, in saddles, or on low-pitched roofs. Normal felt underlayment should still be installed in non-critical areas, and metal flashing should still be used, as per ordinary roof installation.

Waterproofing shingle underlayment must be installed over bare sheathing. Installation is a two-man job. Unroll the underlayment while your assistant peels off the plastic film backing. Carefully set the material in place. During installation, the material is slightly tacky, but can be lifted and repositioned if necessary. However, once it's installed and exposed to sunlight, the underlayment locks tight.

It's important to know what waterproof shingle underlayment can and cannot do. The underlayment will protect those vulnerable areas of your roof from leaks; it does not prevent the formation of the ice dams that form those leaks. Proper insulation and ventilation of your attic are essential to avoid ice damming in the first place. In addition, since the underlayment is a complete vapor barrier, it can prevent the escape of moisture from your attic. To prevent condensation-related problems, make sure that your attic is adequately ventilated.

Types of Drip Edge

The ends of eaves and rakes often need to be protected by more than just the overhang of the roofing material. Install preformed eaves and rake flashing (called drip edge) along the eaves before underlayment is applied and along rakes after the underlayment is down. Cut corners carefully with a tin snips, both for the sake of appearance and for better coverage. Nail the drip edge to the roof sheathing every 8 to 10 inches. Do not nail the drip edge to the fascia.

Wrap-around end-cap flashing covers the edges of old roofing layers. Be sure flashing overlaps at corners. For example, rake flashing must overlap eaves flashing so water is shed downward without working its way beneath the flashing (A).

For roofing trimmed flush with the fascia, this type of end-cap covers the edges of layers and keeps water and ice from backing under the old shingles (B).

A canted drip edge of this variety carries the water away from the fascia (C).

This type of drip edge is designed to contain pea gravel on a built-up roof (D).

Sometimes called drip cap, this flashing adds a lip to the roof edge that overlaps the gutter (E).

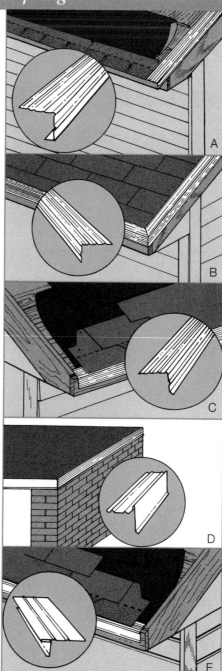

For best results paint galvanized flashing with primer on both sides before installing. Let the flashing run wild (temporarily overhang) past the eaves and the top of the valley. Carefully trim both ends flush after it is nailed in place. Place the nails about 6 inches apart in rows 1/2 inch from the edges. If you need to use more than one piece of metal, nail the first piece at the bottom of the valley and lap the second piece over it by 6 inches. Dab nailheads with roofing cement.

Roll Roofing Valleys. A less costly and less durable option for open valleys is roll roofing. Typically used with asphalt shingles, two layers of roll roofing are applied: One layer is 18 inches wide (the full width of the roll cut lengthwise in half) and one is 36 inches wide (full width). The 18-inch piece is laid granule side down while the 36-inch piece is laid granule side up. Strike a chalk line down the center of each piece to center it in the valley. Nail one side only at first. Before nailing the other side, press the roofing firmly into the valley to eliminate voids that might become punctured later. Mark the valley with chalk lines 6 inches apart at the top of the valley. The bottom is 6 inches wide plus 1/8 inch per foot of descent. The shingles overlap the chalk line and later are trimmed. The uppermost corner of the shingle is nipped diagonally to direct water flow into the valley. A final dab of roofing cement applied after shingles are trimmed keeps water from working under the roofing (see page 44).

Flashing Options

Flashing is available in a variety of forms starting with aluminum coil on the least expensive end of the spectrum and copper sheeting on the most expensive end. Aluminum is readily available in widths ranging from 10 to 36 inches. Colors vary as well with the most typical being white, black and brown.

W-bend galvanized steel flashing is available in 8- to 10-foot lengths, 20 to 24 inches wide. If you would like to bend the flashing for a custom fit, rent a break (a device typically used to neatly bend aluminum siding soffits and trim). They are simple to use and available at most rental shops.

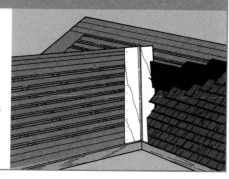

Full-Width Roll Roofing Placed Granules Up

18" Strip of Roll Roofing Placed Granules Down Under Full-Width Roll Roofing

Chalk Line Guides for Shingles

Installing Roll Roofing Valleys. Two layers of roll roofing, one 18-in. wide, the other 36-in. wide, make a nonmetallic valley for use with composition shingles.

Installing Closed Valley Flashing

An extra layer of underlayment is placed in a closed valley. For added protection in harsh climates add a 24-inch-wide sheet of aluminum or galvanized metal. Shingles are laid over the flashing in an alternating fashion or they are half-laced (trimmed down the center of the valley where one plane of shingles overlaps the other).

Installing a Half-Laced Valley. The half-laced (sometimes called half-woven) valley is another type of closed valley. One layer of roofing overlaps the other and is trimmed instead of woven. The overlap is put on the face of the roof that bears the most water. The bottom layer of shingles overlaps the valley by at least 12 inches. After trimming, adhere the topmost layer with roofing cement. No nails are applied within 6 inches of the center of the valley.

Installing Continuous Flashing

Use this simple type of flashing only in places where the joint is horizontal. For example, the joint at which the front wall of a dormer meets the roof, or the place in which a shed roof is attached to a wall. Lay your last course of roofing so that the tops of the shingles butt the wall.

Installing Closed Valley Flashing. Such a valley is woven (or laced) together with courses from either side of the valley alternately overlapping each other. Each overruns the valley by at least a tab and a half.

Installing a Half-Laced Valley. The half-laced valley is a type of closed valley. The overlap is put on the face of the roof that bears the most water.

1 Score the flashing material and sandwich it at the bending point between two 1x4s.

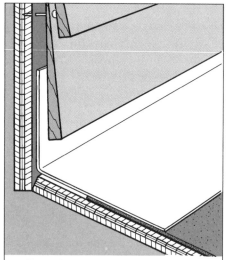

2 Siding overlaps flashing so water sheds downward on top of, not under, the flashing.

3 Cut tabs off shingles and press them into roofing cement applied to the flashing.

If necessary, adjust the exposures in the last two courses so the last course, which will be trimmed to butt the wall, is at least 8 inches wide.

Note: When reroofing it may be possible to continue to use old flashing. If the old flashing is in good repair and you think it will last the life of the new roofing, seal the new roofing to the flashing with roofing cement.

1 **Bending Flashing.** Continuous flashing typically is a strip of metal at least 9 inches wide, bent to match the angle of the joint to be covered. Position the bend so that there will be at least 5 inches of flashing on the wall and 4 inches on the roof. Use clamps and boards to bend the metal neatly. Alternately you can rent a break (typically used to form aluminum soffits and trim caps) to custom-bend aluminum flashing (it does not work for galvanized steel).

2 **Attaching the Flashing.** Put roofing cement on the last course of shingles. On walls that have wood siding, slip the the flashing behind the siding and then press it into the cement. You don't need to nail the flashing to the wall. Nail the flashing to the siding with roofing nails every 2 or 3 feet.

3 **Covering the Flashing.** Cut the tabs off as many shingles as you need for the course. Coat the flashing with roofing cement. Press the tabs into the roofing cement leaving gaps between each that approximate the cutouts between tabs on an intact shingle. Tabs cut from a standard shingle will cover the flashing plus about 1 inch more. Do not nail the tabs. Use a caulk gun to to apply a bead of roofing cement along the flashing junction.

Flashing Brick or Stucco

If the wall is masonry or stucco the job is more difficult because the flashing must be set into the wall.

1 **Bending Lip on Flashing.** Using two boards, clamp the sheet metal or aluminum flashing so that 1/2 inch protrudes freely over the edge. Use a hammer to bend that same 1/2 inch of flashing so that it sticks up at a 90-degree angle.

2 **Cutting the Slot.** Use a piece of chalk to mark a line about 5 inches above the surface of the roof. Use the nearest mortar line if it is a masonry wall. Then use a circular saw (with a masonry blade) or a chisel to cut a 1/2-inch-deep slot along that line. Bend the flashing a second time so that it fits on the roof.

3 **Sealing with Mortar.** Stuff the slot with mortar or silicone caulk and press the top lip of the flashing into the slot.

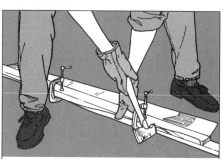

1 Score a line on the flashing and bend the lip as shown.

2 Open the mortar line using a chisel or circular saw with a masonry blade.

3 Fill the chiseled mortar lines with mortar or caulk and set the flashing in place.

Flashing Vents & Soil Stacks

Vents and soil stacks are covered with sleeves. A flap at the base of the sleeve makes a waterproof seal. These sleeves are available in a variety of styles and materials including lead, sheet metal, rubber and plastic. All types are easy to install.

Shingle up to the base of the vent or stack. Cut the shingle around the stack, apply roofing cement and slip on the sleeve (left).

Shingles overlap the upper half of the vent sleeve. Cut the overlapping courses around the stack, leaving a 1/2-inch gap. Cement the tabs to the sleeve (right).

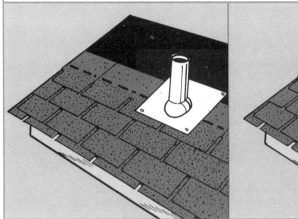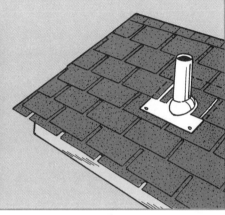

Flashing a Chimney

This job is probably the most complicated part of roofing a house. Old flashing pieces can be used as templates, but keep in mind that by reroofing or tearing off the old roof, the dimensions of the flashing have changed. Chimney flashing typically consists of base flashing (which wraps the front of the chimney), step flashing (which is placed up the sides of the chimney), cricket flashing (a peaked piece that diverts water from the upslope side of the chimney) and pieces of counter flashing (also called cap flashing which hangs over all the other flashing pieces).

If the chimney is 24 inches or wider construct a cricket along the upper side of the chimney. This helps keep water and snow from building up in this critical area.

Before flashing, complete all final roofing up to the base of the chimney and no further.

Step Flashing

Use step flashing on a shingled roof where the roof meets the sloping side of a wall or a chimney. (For roll or panel roofing use continuous flashing). Step flashing requires that each piece of flashing overlaps the one below it. The flashing is interlaced with the shingles as well. You can purchase step flashing precut or you can cut the flashing into shingle-like pieces 10 inches long and 2 inches wider than the exposure of the roofing. For example, if the shingle exposure is 5 inches each shingle is cut 10x7 inches. Install the flashing so that it has the same exposure as the shingles, nailing the the top edge into the roof only so the nails are covered by shingles.

In the illustration at right, the roofing exposure (the amount of roofing material visible in each course) is 5 inches.

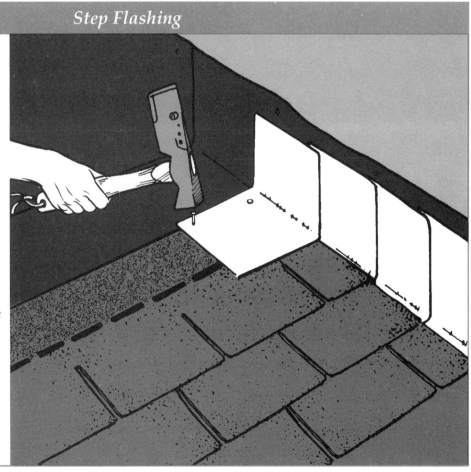

1 Adding Base Flashing. Base flashing is applied at the base of the chimney. Make your own by bending a piece of aluminum with a straightedge. For a simple jig to make this bend and to add a lip to the flashing, see page 28. After bending the aluminum, mark where it intersects the open mortar line and bend a lip along the upper edge. Wearing gloves, use tin snips to cut wings that wrap around the sides of the chimney. Seal the lip of the flashing in the mortar line with mortar or caulk. Overlap the roofing with the lower edge of the flashing.

2 Applying Step Flashing. Install step flashing as you shingle the roof, nailing it as shown on page 29. Cement each step to the roof but not the chimney as the roof may settle independently.

3 Fitting Counter Flashing. Counter flashing is a layer that sheds water onto step flashing. With a large sheet of paper make a template, or have one made by a sheet metal shop that stair-steps down according to mortar lines. The lips of the flashing are set 1/4 inch into the mortar line. Trace the outline onto the sheet metal and cut it with tin snips. Use the edge of a screwdriver to score the lines along which the lips bend. Use two scraps of wood to clamp and bend the lips. Set the finished flashing in place, mortaring or caulking the lips into the chimney. Do not connect the counter flashing to the other flashing pieces because the roof and the chimney are on different foundations and thus settle independently. Do not smear the bottom pieces with caulk or roofing cement because this attaches them to both roof and chimney.

4 Adding a Cricket. A cricket keeps water, snow and debris from piling up behind a chimney. The height of the cricket is one half the width of the chimney. Crickets are made of wood that is roofed over or sheet metal exposed as flashing. Given a sketch of what is needed, a sheet metal shop will cut and break a cricket for you. If you are going to do it yourself, the simplest approach is to add a 2x6 frame behind the chimney. One 2x6 is cut on an angle so it can be nailed horizontally with a second stub piece to support it at the chimney. Two scraps of 1/2-inch CDX plywood cut to incline at roughly 45 degrees form a miniature roof. To finish the job apply felt, flashing and roll roofing.

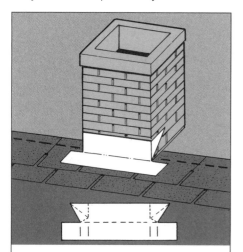

1 Cut the base flashing and use roofing cement to carefully attach it to the roofing.

2 Install the step flashing as the roofing is applied to the chimney.

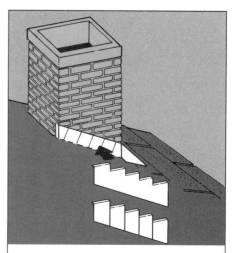

3 Set counter flashing into the mortar line in overlapping sections or in one continuous piece.

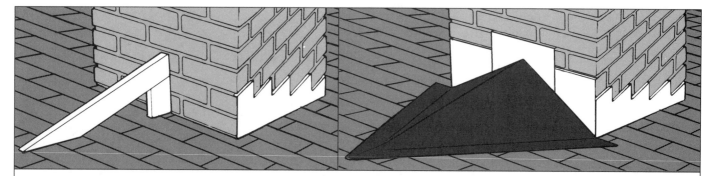

4 Framing for a cricket consists of no more than one horizontal ridge piece supported by one vertical piece (left). Nail two pieces of 1/2-in. plywood to the ridge piece and the deck . Install flashing, then cover with roll roofing (right). Allow the roll roofing to overlap the roof by 4 or 5 inches.

COMPOSITION SHINGLES

Asphalt shingles, also known as composition shingles, are the most common roofing material in North America. Since they are simple to apply and require few specialized tools, they are an ideal material for the do-it-yourselfer.

Selecting Composition Shingles

Shingles are purchased by the square which is enough shingles to cover 100 square feet at the recommended exposure. Shingles typically are packaged 80 to the square, though larger shingles are packaged 64 to the square. Each square is made up of bundles of paper-wrapped blocks of shingles. Most squares are made up of three bundles, but heavier squares are made up of four.

The durability of shingles used to be rated by the weight of the square. The heavier the square, the thicker and longer-lived the shingle. Today shingles are given lifetime ratings of 15, 20 and 25 years. Prices rise accordingly. Colors include white, black, and shades of brown, green, gray and blue. Pressed texture and granule coloration combine to produce shingles that resemble wood shingles and shakes.

When selecting a color remember that roofs last 20 years, far longer than the latest fashion trends. Neutral blacks, whites, and grays remain the most popular colors.

Composition shingles can be applied to any roof that has a pitch of 4 in12 (4 inches rise for every 12 inches of run) or more. With double felt underlayment, they can be applied to a roof with a pitch as low as 2 in 12 if shingle tabs are sealed down.

Deciding to Reroof

Composition shingles are a versatile material and can be used to cover almost anything that accepts a nail.

Composition Shingles. Nail down warped shingles and fill voids. Usually only three layers of shingles are allowed; check your local codes.

Wood Shingles. Add thin, beveled strips (called horse feathers) to fill the voids between courses, and notch in 1x4s at the rakes and eaves to create a smooth platform for a new layer of roofing.

Roll Roofing. If the pitch is at least 4 in 12, roll roofing makes a smooth bed for a new layer of composition shingles. Remove all loose nails before reroofing.

Tile and Slate Roofs. Tile and slate roofs, as well as metal and fiberglass panels, are impossible to nail through and therefore cannot be reroofed with composition shingles. Shakes are too uneven to take new roofing and must be removed as well.

Estimating Materials on Gabled Roofs

You need to be able to tell your local lumberyard or roofing supplier how many squares (100 square feet) of roofing you need. By determining the square footage of your roof, and adding 10 percent for ridges and waste, you can estimate costs and order materials. It is safest and most convenient to take as many measurement as you can from the ground. With a simple gable roof, you can take all the measurements without a ladder. But you'll have to climb up to directly measure details such as dormers. Here's how to measure your roof with little or no climbing:

Different Types of Composition Shingles

Composition shingles come in a variety of styles and colors to complement the architectural and color scheme of your house. Here are three of the most common composition shingle styles you will find.

Standard Three-Tab Shingles. These are the most common style in North America today. They typically are sold 80 shingles per square, three bundles per square (left).

Shadow Line Three-Tab Shingles. The illusion of thickness is created by a line of darkened granules. These too come 80 shingles per square, three bundles per square (center).

Mock Wood Shakes. Added thickness and the clever use of color give mock wood shingles their wood-like appearance. Because they are thicker and heavier, they are sold only 64 shingles per square, four bundles per square (right).

1 **Sketching the Roof.** From the ground make a rough sketch of your roof. Include all planes of the roof including valleys, dormers and chimneys. Do not worry about getting it to scale. Next, reduce the diagram to a series of triangles, rectangles and squares, drawing in dotted lines where appropriate. (Later these shapes are calculated for area.)

2 **Measuring Gable and Eaves Lengths.** First measure the length of your house on one of the eaves sides. Include the gable overhang in your measurement. To determine how far the overhangs protrude, stand directly under them and measure to the house. This will give you a rough measurement of the length of the eaves, but close enough for estimating materials. Mark the eaves length on your drawing.

Now measure the width of the gable end, again including gable overhangs. Jot down this measurement, but don't put it on the drawing yet.

3 **Measuring Pitch.** The purpose of the next two steps is to deter-

1 To determine the area of the roof, sketch a simple bird's eye view. Divide the plan into squares, rectangles and triangles.

2 Measure the length of the eaves end and gable end of your house. Include the eaves and gable overhangs in your measurement.

3 Use a level and a ruler to determine the pitch of your roof.

mine the length of the rake which is one-sloped edge of your roof. When you know the length of the rake and the length of the eaves, you can multiply them to get the square footage of your roof.

First, calculate the pitch of the roof. Pitch is expressed as inches of roof rise (unit rise) per 12 inches of roof run (unit run). A 6 in 12 roof rises 6 inches per 12 inches of run. The pitch of the roof is determined from the ground by using a spirit level and a ruler. Mark the level 12 inches from one end. Stand back from a gable and hold the level so that one end appears to touch the eaves. Make sure the level is exactly horizontal. At the 12-inch mark on the level hold the ruler upright and note the number of inches to the rake. This is the rise. Almost all house pitches are expressed in whole inches. For example, 4 in 12, 6 in 12, etc.

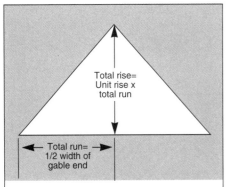

4 From the length of the gable and the pitch of the roof, calculate the total rise of the gable.

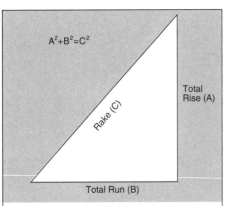

5 From the length of the gable and it's total rise, you can determine the length of the rake.

4 Determining Total Rise. Let us say for example that the gable end of your house is 20 feet wide including the overhangs. That means the base of the triangle you are calculating, or the total run of the roof, is 10 feet long. Let us also assume you have determined that the pitch is 6 in 12. This means that in a total run of 10 feet, the roof rises 5 feet.

5 Calculating Rake Length. This is an opportunity to put your high school geometry to use. Remember the Pythagorean Theorem? This useful formula asserts that if you know the measurements of two sides of a right triangles, the third can be computed. This means that if you know the length of a gable (which you measured from the ground) and you know its height, you can determine the length of the rake .

The total rise squared times the total run squared gives us the length of the rake squared. In our example, the 10-foot total run squared equals 100. The 5-foot total rise squared equals 25. Added together they equal 125, which is the rake squared. The square root of 125 is 11.18, so the rake is 11 feet $2\frac{1}{8}$ inches long. Now multiply the rake length by the length of the eaves. Then you have the area of one side on the gable roof.

6 Calculating the Area. If you are dealing with a simple gable roof with no dormers, just double the area of one side of the roof and add 10 percent for waste and ridge cap

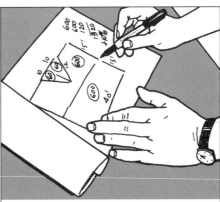

6 With the measurements in place, you can calculate the total area of your roof.

shingles. Divide the square footage by 100 for the total number of squares needed. If your rake is 11.18 feet long and your eaves end is 40 feet long, one side of your roof will be 447.2 square feet. Both sides will be 894.4 square feet. You need nine squares to cover the roof. Adding 10 percent, you should order 10 squares.

If you have dormers, climb up on the roof and measure their length and width directly. When all measurements are determined, compute the area of each roof plane using the following formulas: One side of a rectangle or square multiplied by an adjacent side yields the area; the area of a right triangle equals one half the base multiplied by the height. Again, total all areas and add 10 percent for waste and extras. Do not subtract for chimneys, air vents, and small skylights. Then divide by 100 for the total number of squares needed.

You'll need one 36-inch x 144-foot roll of felt underlayment per three squares of shingles.

Storing Shingles

Composition shingles have adhesive blobs that, when warmed by the sun, seal each tab. For this reason shingles must be stacked out of the sun. Bundles also must be protected from the rain. Shingles are best stored on a skid and covered with plastic.

The most physically demanding part of roofing is getting the shingles on the roof. Many suppliers offer this service which is well worth the additional expense (right).

If the job is going to be spread over several evenings and weekends, carry up only as many shingles that can be applied in a day. Partial bundles can be carried across one's padded head, or whole bundles can be supported on one padded shoulder (center right). Most shingle bundles weigh about 75 pounds.

If you would rather not carry the shingles up by hand, use a ladderveyor (below). Be sure to read the ladder safety tips found on pages 7-9.

A bundle set on either side of the ridge forms a level base for stacking additional bundles. Doing this provides an open work area (below right).

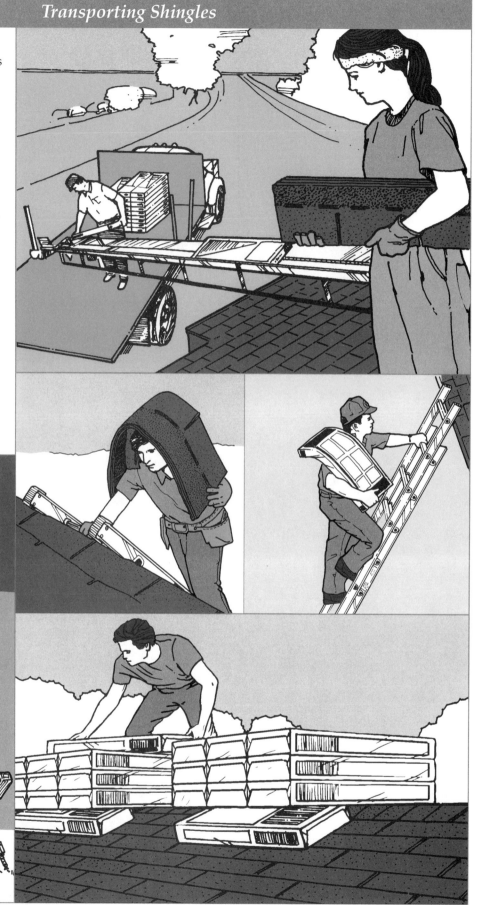

Installing the Starter Course

Composition shingles overlap each other, covering the roof with two layers of roofing. To provide the first layer at the eaves edge, a starter course is applied. The starter course is always necessary whether reroofing over old shingles, applying shingles on a new roof or applying shingles after a tear-off. The procedure is different for reroofs than it is for a new roof or tear-off.

Working with a Reroof

Adding Drip Edge. If shingles at the edge of the eaves are deteriorated cut them back flush with the fascia or old drip edge below. Add a metal drip edge to prevent moisture from getting under the shingles. This protects the fascia boards from rot and provides a finished appearance and a straight, strong edge. Apply the drip edge with roofing nails.

Applying Reroof Starter. When reroofing, the starter strip is just wide enough to cover the exposure of the first course of old shingles. Make a starter strip by cutting the tabs off of several shingles. The resulting strip is 4 to 5 inches wide.

Trim 3 inches off one side of the first strip so that no joints between strips fall over joints between old roofing shingles. Nail it in place with four nails at 3 or 4 inches above the eaves edge. If you added a drip edge bring the edge of the starter course even with the edge of the drip edge. If you did not use a drip edge allow the starter strip to extend 1/4 to 3/8 inch beyond the edge of the eaves.

Starting a New Roof or Tear-Off

Apply a starter course directly on top of the roofing felt. Simply use full shingles that have been flipped around so that the bottom of the tabs are reversed. Trim 3 inches off one side of the first shingle so joints are staggered rather than lined up with the first course of shingles below. Staggering joints prevents leaks. Apply the starter course so that it is flush with the drip edge. If there is no drip edge allow the starter strip to overhang the edge of the eaves by 1/4 to 3/8 inch.

Adding Drip Edge. If the edges of existing shingles are deteriorated cut them back and add a drip edge.

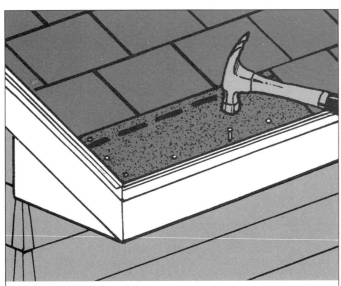

Applying Reroof Starter. Trim the tabs off several shingles for starter strips.

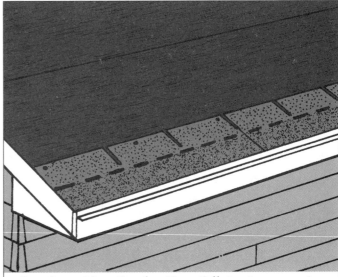

Starting a New Roof or Tear-Off. Apply reversed whole shingles. Trim off 3 in. to stagger the joints.

Starter Strips. These are available in rolls that are simple to install.

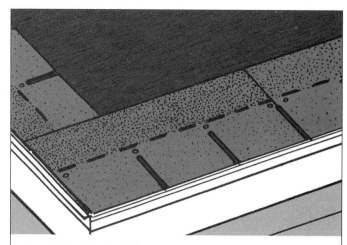

Applying Rake Edge. If the rake edge is badly worn, nail whole shingles, upper edge out, along the rake.

Starter Strips. As an option, starter strips can be purchased in rolls which are simply rolled out and nailed down. There are no joints so you do not have to worry about staggering. Nail every 10 or 12 inches, 3 to 4 inches above the eaves edge. If you live in an area subject to heavy snowfalls or driving rain you might want to add roll products that inhibit ice dams.

Applying Rake Edge. If the rake edge (the roof edge above the gable) is badly deteriorated, supplement the new shingles with a border of whole shingles applied along the rake edge. Keep the upper edge of the shingle toward the rake edge with tabs inward. Allow 1/4- to 3/8-inch overhang. Nail every 10 to 12 inches, 3 to 4 inches in from the edge.

Applying the First Courses

The edge of the roof does not follow a straight line in most cases and cannot be used as a guide for straight courses of shingles. All of the first course shingles must overhang the drip edge by the same 1/4 to 3/8 inch so it is okay to align the first course to the drip edge and then snap a chalk line to align the second course. Make a mark near both rakes to indicate how far up the roof you want the bottom of the course to be. Hold the chalk receptacle downward to fully coat the line with chalk. Then stretch the line taut across the two marks, pull up on it and release to make the line.

You'll be working on an extension ladder to install the starter course along the eaves. While you are installing the starter course, add four more courses along the eaves to provide room for roof cleats. By doing these courses along with the starter course, you'll minimize the number of times you have to move the ladder. While up there, renail and adjust gutter hangers as necessary.

Applying The First Courses. The edge of the roof may not be straight so you must snap a chalk line to establish a straight second course.

Tips for Fastening

Whether you choose to hammer nails or apply staples driven by a pneumatic gun, the following tips help to achieve a secure fastening job:

Use zinc-coated nails to prevent corrosion.

■ Avoid exposing fasteners. Each row of shingles must cover the fasteners of the previous course.

■ Do not drive the fastener so deep that its head breaks the surface of the shingle.

■ A nail that penetrates too easily may work its way out. Remove it and seal the hole.

■ Always drive fasteners in straight so that the heads lay flat. Nail heads that stick up at an angle can wear through the shin-gle above.

■ If the fastener does not penetrate properly remove it, patch the deck, and drive another fastener nearby.

■ Do not nail into or above an adhesive strip.

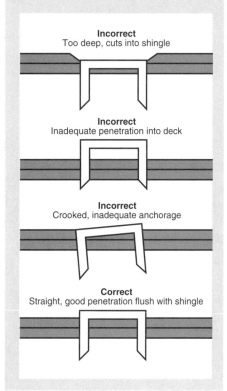

Incorrect
Too deep, cuts into shingle

Incorrect
Inadequate penetration into deck

Incorrect
Crooked, inadequate anchorage

Correct
Straight, good penetration flush with shingle

Nailing Shingles Properly

Shingles are typically attached with four nails; one at each end and one above each tab slot. In windy areas some roofers use six nails, adding one to either side of each tab slot. Note that nails are positioned just beneath the adhesive, but above the tops of the slots. Nails also must be long enough to penetrate the sheathing by 3/4 inch. This rule applies whether fastening the shingles to a new roof or to a reroof.

Basic Shingling

Nothing is more frustrating than hammering four to six nails into a shingle only to find that it is crooked. The procedure below will help you get the shingle aligned right the first time.

1 **Lining Up the Shingle.** Begin by aligning the upper corner of the shingle with the upper corner of the shingle already in place. Tack a nail to hold it in place.

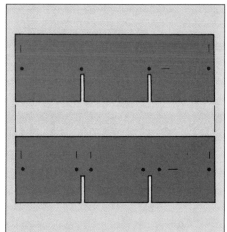

Nailing Shingles Properly. Either 4 or 6 nails are used to hold shingles. Nail in the pattern shown above.

2 **Tacking Opposite End.** Position the opposite end of the shingle. (Some people do this by simply eyeballing where the tab hits the shingle on the previous course. Others use the gauge built into a roofing hammer.) Tack in place.

3 **Checking and Nailing.** Give the shingle a quick double-check for alignment. Then, beginning from the left (if you are right-handed)

1 Align the upper corner of the new shingle with the upper corner of the adjacent shingle.

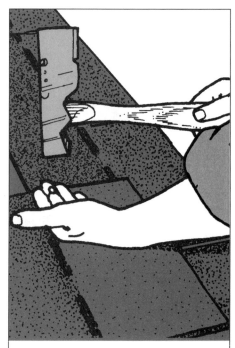

2 Position the opposite edge of the shingle and tack it in place.

nail the first tacked nail home and work across the course, carefully flattening out bulges. If necessary, remove one of the tacked nails to eliminate buckling.

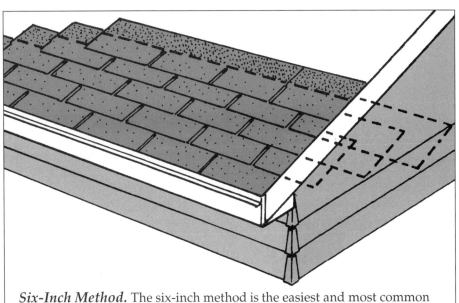

Six-Inch Method. The six-inch method is the easiest and most common shingling pattern. Alternating tab cutouts are aligned.

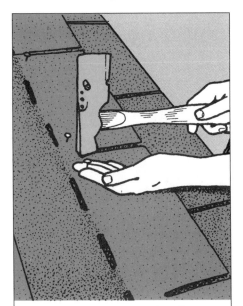

3 Drive in the tacked nails across the shingle.

Choosing a Shingle Pattern

Before nailing skills are put to work, you must choose a shingle pattern. Each pattern requires standard three-tab shingles which are positioned differently to achieve different effects. Each offsets the tab cutouts of overlapping courses by a different distance.

Six-Inch Method. The most common method of aligning shingles is called the six-inch method. Each course starts at a 6-inch offset to the course below. This is handy because it neatly cuts tabs in half and therefore minimizes waste. The result is a neat arrangement where each tab lines up with the tab two courses above or below.

Four- and Five-Inch Methods. Though the six-inch method is the easiest to cut and apply, some theorists are concerned with the way every other vertical cutout lines up and as a result creates a flow path that may erode shingles. This issue is still being debated, but there are other patterns that avoid the prob-

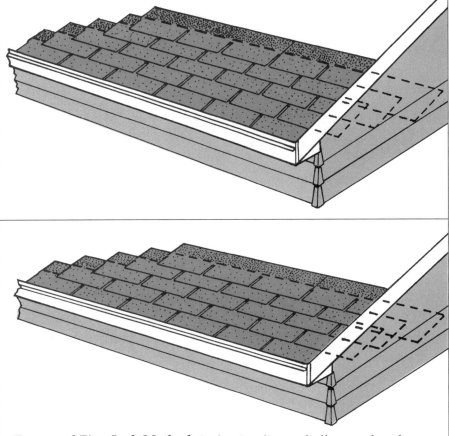

Four- and Five-Inch Method. A pleasing diagonal effect results when shingles are trimmed in 5 in. increments (top). The four-inch method is even more abruptly diagonal. Tab cutouts align vertically only every fourth course (bottom).

lem altogether. The five-inch method provides a bit more offset and more of a diagonal pattern to the shingles.

The four-inch method is diagonal in appearance with two full shingles between tab slots.

Choosing to Hammer

Professional roofers who nail by hand are a vanishing breed. As a do-it-yourselfer you have two options. If you are able to set aside a block of time to complete the roof in one go you can rent a pneumatic stapler (ask the rental dealer to demonstrate safe use of the equipment). However, renting equipment results in added expenses and the additional time it takes to learn how to use that equipment. Breaking out a simple hammer is often the better choice. The following is a professional nailing technique that speeds a hammering job along.

Holding a Handful. Hold a dozen or so nails loosely in your hand. Using only one hand work a nail around so it hangs head up between your fingers. (left)

Hammering the Nail Home. Position the nail on the shingle using the nail hand only. Nail it. (center)

Working Nails into Position. While one hand is nailing the other hand is busy readying the next nail. (right)

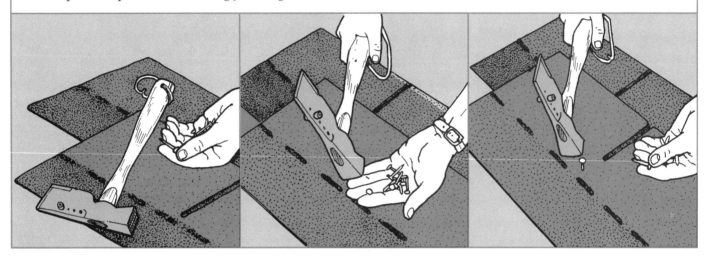

Using a Roofing Hammer

A roofing hammer speeds up any roofing job and although it is a relatively expensive tool, it is worth the investment if you are doing a large roofing job. A roofing hammer's heavy weight is an advantage for quickly whacking nails home, but be careful of its serrated head which is especially hard on fingers if you miss the nail.

With a built-in course gauge set according to the exposure desired, this hammer is far more precise and much faster than simply eyeballing the top of the shingles. The guide pin can be set in any one of the several holes for the desired course depth (left).

Hook the pin on the course below and let the bottom edge of the shingle rest against the heel of the hammer (center).

The hatchet side of the hammer is designed for splitting wood shingles to size (right). It is less useful for composition shingles, but is still good for chopping out old roofing cement or flashing.

Random Shingling. With random shingling each course is offset a multiple of 3 inches. The order of the multiples—whether they be 3, 6, 9, or 12 inches of offset—varies. The effect is a helter-skelter look with some of the character of random-width wood shingles or slates.

Shingling a Stair-Step Pattern

At this point the roof is prepared for shingling, the shingles are ordered, and the shingling pattern has been chosen. The following is a step-by-step approach to the six-inch pattern. Except when it comes to the amount of shingle that must be trimmed, the same instructions apply to the other shingling patterns .

Rather than working across the roof one row at a time (and moving ladders, cleats, etc. each time) experienced roofers stair-step as many courses as they can safely reach—and as far across as roof brackets permit. By building up a stair-step pattern of shingles along the left-

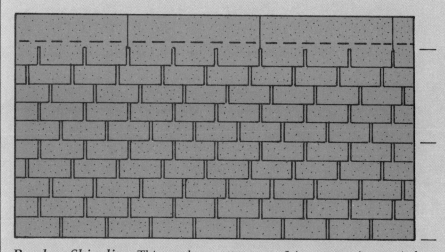

Random Shingling. This random pattern uses 3-in. cutouts in a varied order to achieve a look similar to wood shingles or slate.

hand eaves of the roof (left-handed shinglers work from the right side of the roof), you can add on a series of whole shingles without moving the roof cleats.

1 Precutting Shingles. Set up a work area on the ground. A 4x4 scrap of plywood on a sawhorse is ideal. Using an angle square and a utility knife equipped with a roofing hook blade, cut a series of partial

shingles so you can stair-step up five courses. (Save scrap pieces for possible use as filler at the opposite end of the roof.)

2 Starting the Course. The first shingles are placed over the eaves course (the first course of shingles laid on top of the starter course). Double-check to be sure seams between shingles do not line up with seams in the starter course.

1 A stair-step pattern starts each course with a shingle half a tab less than the course above.

2 To assure that cutouts align vertically use the alignment notches along the tops of the shingles.

3 Stair-step the pieces in place along the rake edge.

4 Measure every 12 courses or so to check that courses are running parallel to the eaves.

3 **Building the Stair-Step.**
Remove one half of a tab from a shingle and use this shingle to begin the second course. If you are using a roofing hammer use the gauge to keep course depth consistent. Continue adding partial shingles along the rake to achieve the stair-step pattern. Once the pattern is complete you can add course after course of whole shingles.

4 **Checking and Aligning.**
Almost all composition shingles have alignment notches in the middle of each tab along the upper edge of the shingle. These are especially useful when beginning courses. Pinch one side of the alignment notch upright so the new shingle butts against it. Roofs seldom are perfectly square. If correction is needed strike a chalk line as a guide for the next course.

Nesting

When applying new shingles directly over the old, the roof first must be brushed to remove any debris or loose granules. New shingles are

then "nested" over the old shingles. This maintains the old exposure and provides a quick way to align the new shingles because you push the tops of the new shingles against the bottom tabs of the old. The result is a smooth, uniform covering.

Nesting is simple. Begin by trimming the tabs off a whole shingle to make a starter strip. It fits just between the

eaves edge and the bottom of the second course of shingles. Note that the tab adhesive provides a good seal at the eaves. In positioning the starter strip be sure to adequately overlap tab cutouts on the first course of the old roof. Once the starter strip is in place proceed with the courses, positioning them so that cutouts offset the old cutouts by 3 inches.

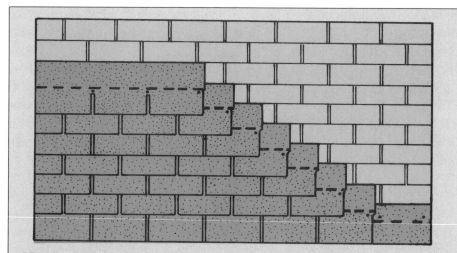

Nesting. The nesting method of applying new shingles over old provides even coverage and quick course alignment.

Ribbon Courses

A ribbon course adds interest to the standard six-inch pattern.

After six courses have been applied cut a 4-inch-wide strip lengthwise off the upper section of a shingle. Nail it as the seventh course 1/4 inch below the top of the cutouts of the sixth course. Then reverse the 8-inch-wide leftover scrap and nail it on top of the 4-inch strip (top). Cover both with the next full course. Doing this creates a three-ply edge also known as the ribbon (bottom).

Working on Steep Roofs

It is extremely difficult to work on a high-pitched roof. A scaffold is a necessity in these situations. Unless you own a scaffold and are experienced in using it, it's best to hire a contractor to handle steep roofs.

Roofs that exceed a pitch of 21 in 12 (a mansard roof is likely to have this sort of pitch) render factory-applied, self-sealing adhesive ineffective. This is because the extreme pitch makes it impossible for heat and gravity to complete the seal. In this case use extra sealant. Put a quarter-size dab of quick-setting roofing cement under each tab as you shingle. Also, apply six fasteners to each shingle: One at either end and two above and to either side of each tab cutout.

Working on Low Slopes

Water tends to be blown under shingles applied to low slopes so special precautions must be taken. Where the rise is 2 to 4 inches in 12, use square-tab shingles with double underlayment and roofing cement. (A roof with a pitch less than 2 in 12 cannot be covered with tab shingles. Use roll or built-up roofing instead.) Apply a double thickness of underlayment, lapping each course over the preceding one by 19 inches. Start with a 19-inch strip at the eaves. If you live in a cold climate protect against ice dams by cementing together the two felt layers up to a point 2 feet inside the interior wall line of the house.

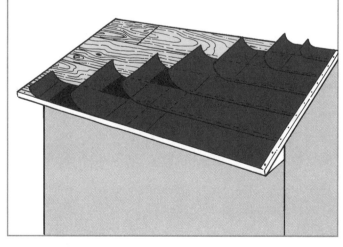

Roofing the Valleys

Valleys are among the most difficult and most important areas to roof. A valley forms the junction between two planes on a roof and must carry off a great deal of water. The two types of valleys are called open and closed. Open valleys create a channel down which water flows. Closed valleys are shingled over completely. The valley is the most vulnerable section of a roof. During a torrent, water is sometimes driven under shingles on either side of the valley, causing leaks. Always avoid stepping in a valley when working on the roof.

Building Open Valleys

1 Applying Roll Roofing. Fill in the valley with an 18-inch piece of roll roofing. Roll out the length needed from a 36 inch-wide roll. Then flip it over, strike a line at 18 inches and cut with a utility knife. Roll it up again before carrying it up to the roof.

Coat the valley with roofing cement and lay the piece of roll roofing granule-face down. Drive a nail every 12 inches down one side. Nail the other side after nesting the piece completely into the valley, leaving no voids beneath. Then center a full-width (36-inch) piece over it, granules down. Nail along one edge only. Let the roofing run wide, which means you just let extra lengths of roofing flop over the ridge and eaves to be trimmed later. Split the roofing at the ridge and eaves so it lays flat.

Trim the lower edge flush with the eaves and cut a slight radius at the inside corner on the intersection of the eaves.

2 Shingling and Trimming. Use a chalkline to mark the center of the valley. Continue installing shingles until they reach the valley. Make sure the last shingle in each course ends within 3 inches of the centerline. Then strike guidelines for trimming the shingles. Start the lines 6 inches apart at top and let them diverge 1/8 inch per foot toward the eaves.

3 Nipping Corners. Slip a scrap of roofing under the shingles and trim the new shingles using a utility knife with a hook blade. Be careful not to pierce the roll roofing. When one side is completely trimmed work your way back up the other side, trimming the uppermost corner of each shingle. This prevents the corner from catching water and pulling it under the shingle.

4 Nailing and Cementing Shingles. Nail the shingles at least 4 inches from the trim edge. Use roofing cement to seal down the shingles.

1 Open valleys have a central channel of doubled roll roofing laid granule face down.

Chalk Line

2 After shingling the roof, snap a chalkline to trim the valley.

3 Use a utility knife to trim the uppermost corner off each shingle along the valley.

4 Shingles are cemented to each other and to the roll roofing in the valley.

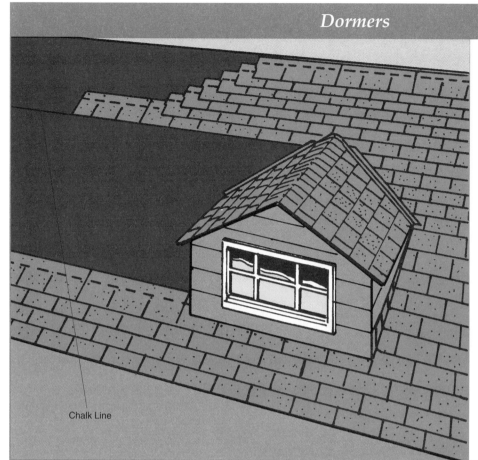

Chalk Line

As the valley leads you up one side of the dormer you probably are wondering how to evenly match the courses of shingles on the other side. Once you have worked your way to a dormer and have completed one valley, continue the topmost course past the ridge of the dormer. Chalk a line that extends the course. If possible check the trueness of the extended line by measuring down from the roof ridge. Nail along the top of the course only so that shingles may be slipped under it later.

Once the course is extended about 10 feet strike parallel chalk lines 36 inches apart to serve as a guide for aligning cutouts as the other side of the dormer is shingled. As you complete shingling on the other side of the dormer, check course alignment as well. Fortunately shingles are a forgiving material and slight adjustments, if made over several courses or shingles, are not noticeable.

Building Closed Valleys

Closed valleys have no channel and are created by continuing the roofing material across the valley. A woven valley (sometimes referred to as a laced valley) is the quickest type of closed valley to install. A slightly more time-consuming variation is the half-weave valley (sometimes called closed-cut or half-laced valley) in which the overlapping layer of roofing is neatly trimmed.

Both types begin with one layer of 36-inch-wide roll roofing. Hold the roll roofing in place with temporary nails tapped lightly into the surface 1 inch from the outer edge of the valley (the nails from the shingles fasten it permanently later). Be careful to work roofing into the valley cavity. This job is easier done on a warm day as warm shingles become pliable enough to lay down completely and without voids. Trim excess at eaves. At the ridge allow the piece to flop over the opposite roof face.

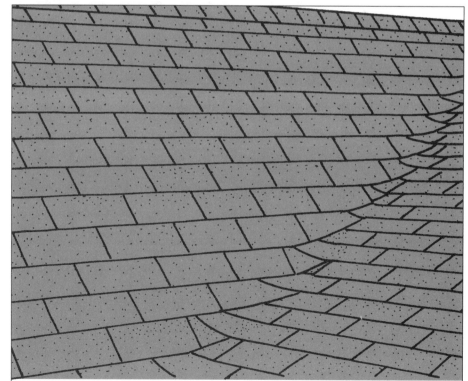

Building Closed Valleys. A woven valley is made up of interlacing shingles from adjacent roof faces. The job is done quickly, but does not offer the best protection or appearance.

Full Weave. In this case overlaps stack up on one side to compensate for the difference in pitch. Do not nail within 6 in. of the centerline of a valley.

Half Weave. One group of shingles is laid across the valley. Shingles on the opposite side are trimmed to bisect the valley with a crisp line.

Full Weave. Complete shingling adjacent planes of the roof that meet at the valley. With a helper, complete the shingling of each plane, weaving the shingles by laying alternate shingles down at each course and pushing them into the valley. Clip the uppermost corner of every overlapping shingle. Apply two nails at the side of the shingle that crosses the valley.

Do not nail within 6 inches of the centerline of a valley. If the pitch of the roof differs on either side of the valley you may have to weave as many as three shingles on one side to one on the other.

Half-Weave. The half-weave valley is a variation on the woven valley. Begin by laying down roll roofing as described. Completely shingle one side of the roof overlapping the valley at least 12 inches beyond the centerline. Next, shingle the opposite side letting the shingles overlap the finished side. Clip the uppermost corner of every overlapping shingle. Do not nail within 6 inches of the centerline of the valley. Strike a chalkline down the center of the valley and trim the shingles. Trim corners nearest the valley and seal shingles with roofing cement.

Air Vents & Plumbing Stacks

Shingling Around Air Vents.
Reroofing (or tearing off and adding a new roof) presents the opportunity to add new air vents to the attic. Old, dented vents also can be replaced while you are on the roof. The roofing principles for handling air vents and plumbing stacks are the same: Flashing covers shingles below the object, shingles overlap the flashing above the object. Air vents overlap all but the topmost shingles. Adhere the vent with a coating of roofing cement.

Shingling Around Air Vents. Install air vents over shingles so that the vent flashing covers all the shingle courses surrounding the hole in the roof. Shingles overlap only the topmost edge of the air vent flashing.

Shingling Around Stacks. The most thorough way to roof around a stack is to remove the flashing. Older homes have lead flashing while newer homes have aluminum or vinyl flashing. (Replacement stack flashing can be readily purchased if the old flashing is damaged.) Continue the courses of roofing beneath the vent, notching them with a utility knife to fit around the pipe. Nail and cement the flashing into place so that it covers the courses below. Continue the courses so that those halfway above the pipe overlap the flashing. Notch them as necessary and seal with roofing cement.

The flashing around a plumbing stack overlaps the same shingles that the stack pierces. Trim an overlapping tab so that it surrounds the stack. Use roofing cement to seal the job.

Shingling Around Stacks. Fit the vent collar onto the stack and over the new roofing. Fasten it with roofing cement. Shingles should overlap only the upper half of the vent collar. Trim the overlapping shingles around the stack, maintaining a 1/2-inch gap. Seal the shingle tabs down with roofing cement.

Shingling Ridges

The ridge of your roof runs from the peak of one gable to the peak of the other. It's the point at which both slopes come together. Here's how to shingle the ridge.

1 **Gang-Cutting Tabs.** Ridges are made by cutting single tabs off of shingles. The easiest way to do this is to stack a bunch of shingles neatly together. Use a square as a guide as you cut through the first shingle to separate the tabs. Taper the cuts slightly as shown in the drawing. Then you can use the top shingle as a guide to slice through the shingles below.

2 **Trimming Final Course.** Wrap ridge shingle piece over the ridge to check whether you need another course of shingles on either slope. Trim the last course of shingles to fit just up to the ridge.

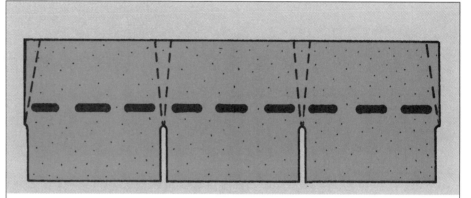

1 Cut single tabs from whole shingles and taper the unexposed area as shown.

2 Apply and trim the final course of shingles. Trim the last course of shingles on each slope to end at the ridge.

A caulk gun loaded with a tube of roofing cement is a handy tool when it comes to finishing up the job. It can be used to seal tabs where roof cleats were suspended, to seal nails on gutter hangers, to coat bolts that hold antennas to the roof, and to seal tabs that may have curled at the edges (bottom).

Strike a chalk line where the shingles overlap the rake by 1/4 to 3/8 inch. Then use a utility knife to trim the rake edges (right)

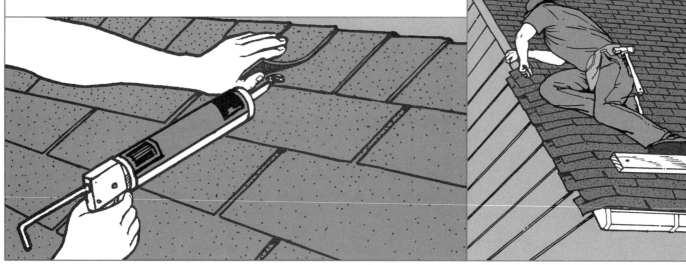

3 Wrapping the Ridge. Strike a chalkline on the most visible side of the house, usually the front. Wrap a single tab over the ridge making sure the alignment notch centers the very apex. Use this as a guide for snapping the line. If there is a prevailing wind direction in your area, work toward it. Apply one nail at either side of each tab and just in front of the sealant line.

4 Topping it off. Nail the final shingle and cover the nail-heads with roofing cement. Seal each tab with roofing cement for a truly windproof ridge.

5 Mitering Ridge Shingles. Begin the ridge of a hip roof with a single tab mitered to suit the shape of the eaves. Position the tab, mark along the eaves line at either side and cut using a square as a guide. Work along the ridge in the same way you would for a gable ridge (see page 47). At the top of the hip ridge, miter adjacent tabs and overlap them with a tab that has been specially cut and folded into a cap.

3 Strike a chalkline and apply the shingles with a 5 in. exposure.

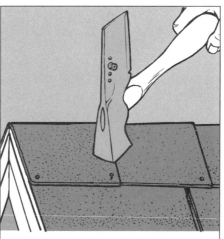

4 To prevent water seepage and wind damage, seal each tab with roofing cement.

5 Use mitered ridge shingles to begin a hip roof ridge and cap it with a cut and folded shingle.

WOOD SHINGLES & SHAKES

Wood shingles and shakes have been used to shelter homes for hundreds of years. Light, long-lasting and beautiful, they are an asset to any home. The installation of shingles and shakes is labor-intensive, so real savings are achieved by doing the project yourself.

Roofing with Wood

Wood shingles and shakes usually are made of Western red cedar, a long-lasting, straight-grained wood. The grain is what gives the wood surprising strength whether it is cut thick or very thin. Even after years of weathering, wood does a much better job of shedding water than might be expected. In addition, wood shingles and shakes resist heat transmission twice as well as composition shingles.

Wood shingles often require more maintenance than other roofing options, especially if you live in a harsh climate. In such areas it is advisable to treat wood shingles and shakes with a preservative every five years or so. Regular cleaning also is recommended to clear away debris that traps moisture and breeds fungus, mildew, rot and insect borers. Wood shingles and shakes are not fire resistant and some local codes may even require that the wood be pressure treated. Some localities have banned wood roofing altogether; be sure to check your local codes before deciding to use wood shingles or shakes. In addition, check with your insurance company to see if your premiums will be affected.

Choosing Between Shingles & Shakes

Shingles are thinner than shakes and are sawn smooth on both sides. Shakes often are split by hand rather than cut and have a very irregular surface. They are thicker and therefore more durable than shingles which typically last no more than 20 to 25 years. There are two common types of shakes used in residential roofing. One type, called tapersplit is split on both sides. Tapersplits are made by hand. The other type, called handsplit and resaw, is split from the block and then sawn to produce two shingles, each with one split and one sawn face.

Straight-split shakes do not taper in thickness (as do all other wood shingles and shakes) and are not intended for residential use.

Both shakes and shingles are available in number 1, 2, and 3 grades. Grade number 1 is cut from heartwood, a clear (knot-free), completely edge-grained wood that is the more resistant to rot than the other grades. It is also the most expensive of the grades. Buy the best grade you can afford. Grade number 2 has a limited amount of sapwood. (Sapwood is less rot-resistant than heartwood.) In addition, number two grade has some knots and is flat grained. It is acceptable for residential roofing. Use grade number 3 shingles or shakes for outbuildings only. Shingles also come in a grade 4 which has large knots and is only acceptable for a starter course. Shakes don't come in grade 4.

The shingle length needed is determined by the desired exposure (the length of shingle exposed to weather). Exposure is determined by pitch. Shingle widths vary from 3 to 9 inches.

Reroofing with Shingles & Shakes

With the proper preparation you can shingle over a roof of wood shingles. However, you cannot shingle over shakes due to their irregular shape. Both shingles and shakes can be installed over composition shingles.

In order to install shingles and shakes the roof must have a large enough slope. The reason for this is simple. Unlike self-sealing composition shingles or roll roofing, voids remain between courses of wood shingles and shakes. With enough pitch for quick runoff this poses no problem, but when installed on a low-slope, roof shingles are not protected from windblown rain and snow.

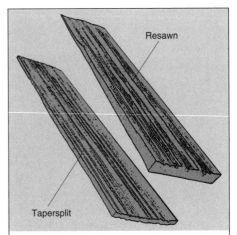

Wooden Shakes. Handsplit and resawn shakes have a split top face and a sawn bottom face. A tapersplit is handmade by splitting on both sides.

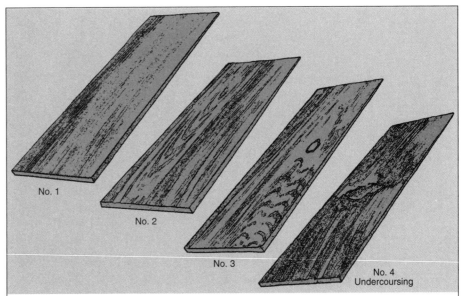

Wooden Shingles. Shingles come in four grades with clear heartwood being the best and undercoursing being the worse.

Shingles are not recommended for roofs with less than a 3 in 12 pitch (see page 33). Shakes are not recommended for roofs with a pitch of less than a 4 in 12. Exposure also must be limited for slight pitches. For example, with a 3 in 12 pitch, 16-inch shingles must have a maximum of 3³/₄-inch exposure (5 inches on 4 in 12 pitch). Eighteen-inch shingles may be exposed a maximum of 4¹/₄ inches (5¹/₂ inches on a 4 in 12 pitch). Shingles that are 24 inches long can have the greatest exposure (5³/₄ inches on a 3 in 12 pitch and 7¹/₂ inches on a 4 in 12 pitch).

Nailing Patterns

Apply shingles and shakes with only two nails per shingle. As the courses overlap four nails pierce each shingle or shake. Place nails about 3/4 inch from each edge and 1 to 2 inches above the lowest edge of the overlapping course. Stagger joints at least 1¹/₂ inches.

Nailing Guides. To keep courses straight, tack a 1x4 guide in place for each course or use the adjustable gauge on a roofing hammer.

Wood shingles and shakes are slippery compared to the gritty grab of composition shingles, so its a good idea to use a toeboard to help keep yourself and your materials on the roof. A toeboard is simply a long 2x4. Use three shakes or shingles as shown to shim the toeboard off the roof, giving you a deeper toe hold. Use 16d or 20d nails through the toeboard, shims, roofing and sheathing and into the rafter below. For a handy place to nest a bundle of shingles, nail two scrap shingles upright on the toeboards. Use a toeboard every 3 or 4 feet up the roof.

A simple seat with a spiked base that grips the newly applied shingles also comes in handy. Build it with plywood and 1x4s. Drill 1/16-inch pilot holes and screw the pieces together with 6x1⅝ galvanized deck screws. Drive roofing nails through the 1x4s before attaching them to the seat The nails stick into the roof to keep you from sliding.

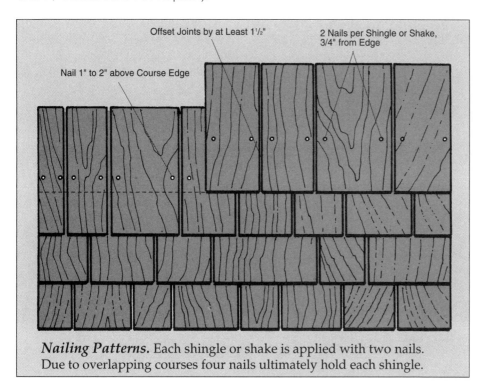

Nailing Patterns. Each shingle or shake is applied with two nails. Due to overlapping courses four nails ultimately hold each shingle.

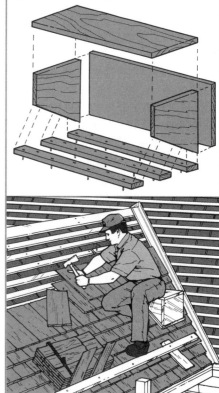

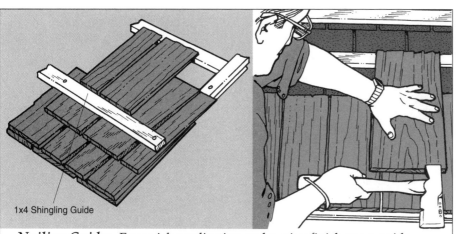

Nailing Guides. For quick application and a crisp finish use a guide board for positioning shingles or shakes (left). A roofing hammer with an adjustable course guide speeds up the job of aligning shingles (right).

Applying Sheathing & Underlayment

Wood roofing benefits greatly from ventilation so it almost always has spaced sheathing. The space allows shingles to dry after rain thereby preventing rot. Solid sheathing, however, still is used at ridges, eaves, rakes, and places exposed to great amounts of wind and snow.

Always use 30-pound felt underlayment when installing shakes. The irregular shape of the shakes allows plenty of air circulation. For wood shingles use underlayment only in areas where ice may collect and at the eaves and rakes.

Before laying shakes (not shingles) nail a drip edge along the eaves.

Begin by laying a full sheet of felt. All subsequent sheets are 18 inches wide. If you cannot purchase 18-inch felt, cut the sheets to size.

When adding a layer of new shingles over old, ventilation channels are made by installing a new underlayment. This process includes removing old shingles, furring out the ridge, renewing the valley flashing and adding a 1x6 nailer at the eaves and rakes.

By adding a similar system of underlayment wood shingles can be installed on top of composition shingles. Trim back the composition shingles where they extend beyond the edge of the roof before installing underlayment.

Covering Wood Shingles

1 Removing the Ridge. Use a flat shovel or crowbar to remove the old ridge.

2 Renewing the Valley. Fur out the valley to bring it to the level of the original shingles. Resurface with new flashing.

3 Reinforcing the Ridge. Beveled siding turned upside down reinforces the ridge and counteracts the bevel of the last course of shingles.

4 Sheathing Rake and Eaves. Use the sharp edge of a roofing hammer to cut away shingles along the rake and eaves. Open a cavity into which a 1x6 piece of sheathing can be nailed.

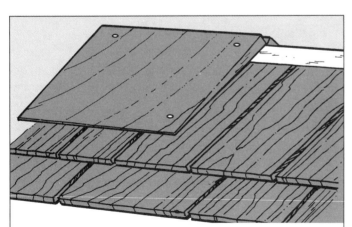

1 The first step in adding a new layer to an old wood roof is to pry off the old ridge with a crowbar or a flat shovel.

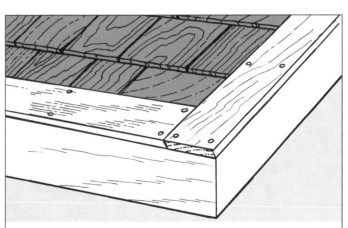

2 Use 1x3s to fill in the valleys so they will be flush with the old roof. Resurface by installing W-metal flashing.

3 Use beveled cedar siding turned upside down to reinforce the ridge and counteract the bevel of the last course of old shingles.

4 Cut away rake and eaves shingles with the sharp edge of a roofing hammer to make room for 1x6 sheathing.

Covering Composition Shingles

1 **Trimming Back.** Use a sharpened roofing hammer to cut away the overhang created by the old composition shingles.

2 **Applying Solid Sheathing.** Using 8d galvanized nails add 1x6 sheathing to provide a solid nailing surface at the ridge, rakes and eaves. Use pairs of 1x3s in the valleys.

3 **Applying Ventilation Strips.** Space 1x3s a distance equal to the desired exposure of the shingles. Metal flashing is applied to the valley before installing shingle courses (see page 52).

1 Trim the old shingles flush to the rake with a utility knife or sharp roofing hammer.

2 Sheathe ridge, rakes, eaves and valley with 1x6 boards fastened with 8d galvanized nails.

3 Ventilation strips, sometimes called "skip" sheathing, allow air to pass between the shingles and the asphalt roof. The strips are made of 1x3s.

Installing Shingles

1 Aligning First Shingles. Lay a starter course that overhangs the eaves by 1 inch. To establish a straight line tack a shingle at either end of the eaves, positioning it so it overhangs the rake by 1/4 to 3/8 inch and the eaves by 1 inch.

2 Lining Up Starter Course. Tack a nail into the butt of each starter shingle at the end of the eaves and run a line between the two. Use the line as a guide for laying the starter course.

3 Adding Courses. Leave 1/8- to 1/4-inch spaces between shingles. Always stagger spaces at least 1 1/2 inches as courses overlap. Snap a chalk line to ensure a straight second course. Set your roofing hammer (if you have one) to the correct exposure and use it as a guide for placing the shingles. Snap a chalk line to check alignment every three or four courses. Use 3d nails for 16- and 18-inch shingles, and 4d for 24-inch shingles. Always use galvanized nails.

4 Cutting Valley Shingles. Use a spare shingle to transfer the angle of the valley to the shingles that will be installed. Align the butt of the shingle at the eaves line, mark the angle and cut. Once you have captured this angle, shingles can be gang cut down on the ground.

5 Using a Guide for Valleys. A piece of one-by carefully placed (not nailed) in the valley provides a simple guide for aligning shingles along the valley. Allow the final course at the top of the roof to extend above the ridge line. Stretch a chalkline even with the ridge line and snap it on the shingles. Score the overhang with a utility knife. Press downward slightly to snap off the excess. Finish hips and ridges with factory-made ridge shingles (see page 56).

1 Install the starter course so they overhang the eaves by 1 inch and the rakes by 1/4 to 3/8 inch.

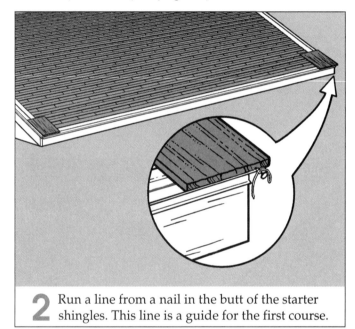

2 Run a line from a nail in the butt of the starter shingles. This line is a guide for the first course.

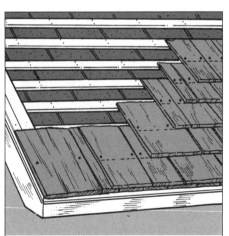

3 Each shingle receives two nails about 3/4 in. from the edge. Use galvanized nails.

4 A spare shingle transfers the angle of the valley to the shingle to be installed.

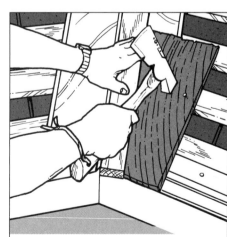

5 A piece of 1x4 laid in the valley simplifies shingle alignment. Do not nail the 1x4.

Installing Shakes

1 **Applying Roll Underlayment.** Unlike shingles, shakes require 18-inch underlayment sandwiched between each course. The underlayment helps shed water and blocks windblown rain. Before laying the first course, install 36-inch-wide, 15- or 30-pound felt underlayment at the eaves. (The felt weight depends on local code). If you live in a climate with a lot of rain and snow it is best to consider shakes only if the roof has a pitch of at least 6 in 12. The irregular pattern that results with shakes provides a major advantage in that you can reroof over composition shingles or solid sheathing. The irregular pattern allows for airflow which is crucial to wood shingles and shakes.

2 **Gauging Each Course.** Shakes are available in 18- and 24-inch lengths. Typical exposures are 7½ inches for 18-inch shakes and 10 inches for 24 inch shakes. You can use your hammer as an exposure guide by measuring up the handle and wrapping a piece of tape around the desired length of exposure.

Begin applying shakes with a doubled starter course that overhangs the eaves by 2 inches and the rakes by 1½ inches. To establish a straight eaves line, tack in place two shakes; one at either end of the eaves. Position each shake so it protrudes 2 inches beyond the drip edge. Hammer a nail into the edge and run a line taut between the two shakes. Each shake just touches the line as the starter course is applied. Set a similar line for the rake. Each shake receives two nails about 3/4-inch from the edge. Use 7d galvanized nails for shakes.

Leave a 1/2-inch gap between shakes. When a course is completed install an 18-inch-wide strip of 30-pound felt underlayment. Position the bottom edge of the felt above the shake butt at a distance equal to twice the weather exposure. Offset the gaps between shingles in neighboring courses by at least 1½ inches.

3 **Marking Valley Shakes.** Lay a spare shake parallel with the valley and over a shake that has been lined up even with the eaves edge. Mark a line and cut the shake. Use this shake as a template for gang-cutting shakes on a table saw.

4 **Using a Guide for Valleys.** A piece of one-by carefully placed (not nailed) in the valley provides a simple guide for aligning shakes that border the valley. Trim underlayment between shake courses to 2 inches short of the guide board.

5 **Extending Final Courses.** Allow the final courses at the top of the roof to extend above the ridge. Snap a chalk line at the ridge height and trim shakes with a circular saw. Finish hips and ridges with factory-made ridge shakes.

1 Begin by installing 36-inch-wide underlayment along the eaves.

2 Install 18-inch wide underlayment between courses of shakes.

3 Use a spare shake to transfer the angle of the valley.

4 Trim underlayment 2 in. short of the 1x4 guide board.

5 Strike a line and use a circular saw to cut shakes at the ridge.

Finishing Shingles & Shakes

1 Installing the Ridge. Precut, factory-made ridge shingles are well worth the money. Begin by striking a line along the side of the ridge that is most visible from the ground. Use ridge shingles at either end of the ridge to set the chalkline. Alternate the mitered joint of the ridge shingles as you work up the ridge.

2 Alternating Overlap. If working on a peak, begin applying the ridge shingles at the end farthest from prevailing weather so that shingles overlap away from the weather. Alternate the overlap of the mitered joint of the precut ridge shingles. On the ridge of a hip roof, double the starter course at the eaves.

3 Nailing Ridge Shingles. Drive two nails into the midpoint of each ridge shingle and just beyond the point of overlap of the next course.

Note: When installing shakes wrap the last course of underlayment over the ridge.

4 Installing Stack Flashing. When applying shingles or shakes around plumbing stacks bring the courses of shingles past the vent and notch them with a keyhole saw or sabre saw. Cut two layers of felt slightly smaller than the base of the stack flashing. The felt fills in variations in the grain. Seal the flashing to the shingles beneath with two layers of 30-pound felt.

5 Notching Shingles Around the Stack. Notch the next course in place. Shingles and shakes permit flexibility around the vent; it is alright for some water to flow beneath the shingles.

6 Surrounding the Stack. With wood shingles (unlike composition shingles) it is possible to completely wrap the stack without causing a back flow. To increase coverage you may choose to drop a shingle down from the final course so that it overlaps the stack flashing.

1 Use ridge shakes to set guides. Then strike a chalk line along the most visible roof plane.

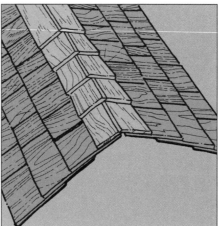

2 Alternate ridge miters to avoid the chance of moisture seepage along the ridge.

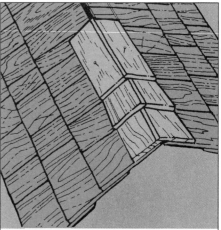

3 Apply two nails: one on each side of the ridge and behind the overlap of the next ridge shingle.

4 Vent flashing overlaps at least one course. Nail the upper edge to the sheathing only.

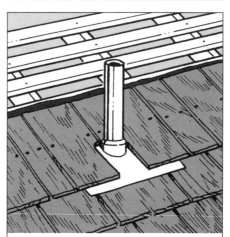

5 Overlap the stack flashing, notching shingles 1 in. from the stack.

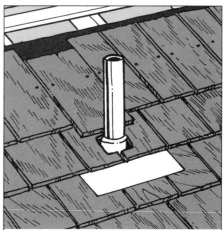

6 Notching is allowed as water flow escapes beneath the shingles and on top of the flashing.

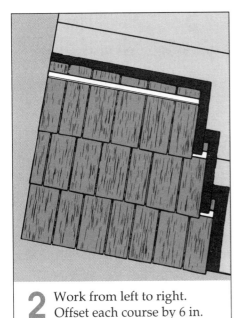

1 Two layers of panels form the starter course.

2 Work from left to right. Offset each course by 6 in.

Panelized Shingles

Wood shingles and shakes are available in prebonded panels, and although they are more expensive than regular shingles and shakes, they also are much quicker to install. Manufacturers claim that panels are installed twice as fast as composition shingles and four times faster than individual shakes or shingles. The panels are glued together in two- and three-ply sections that are 8 feet long. The panels are available in exposures ranging from 5½ inches (for shingles) to 9 inches (for shakes). They are applied on roofs with pitches that are 4 in 12 or greater. Each panel has a score line that is used to align courses. One fastener per shingle or shake holds each panel in place (7 fasteners per panel).

1 Applying Starter Course.
If the roofing is to be applied directly over sheathing, first cover the sheathing with an underlayment of 15-pound felt. (Skip the felt if you are covering composition shingles.) Apply two layers of panels for the starter course, overhanging the eaves by 1½ inches and the rake by 2 inches. Nail the first layer of the starter course with two nails halfway up both ends. Then remove the felt backing from panels to be used on the second layer and nail them in place with seven nails, offsetting them by at least 1½ inches. Use No. 13 gauge, 7/32-inch-head, rust-resistant nails or 2-inch-long,

7/16-inch crown corrosion-resistant staples. Because the felt backing of the panels extends 4 inches on the right side of each panel, they must be laid from left to right.

2 Applying Additional Courses.
Offset the second and subsequent courses by 6 inches. Trim 6 inches off the first panel of the second course, 12 inches off the third course, 18 inches off the third course and so on. The seventh course panel will be about 7 inches long. Save the trimmings—they can be used on the opposite rake. Each panel is scribed at the exposure line for a quick and easy guideline.

3 Trimming Valleys. Cover valleys with 36-inch felt and lay down W-metal valley flashing (see page 25). Trim courses as they are applied so that they are at least 1½ inch from the centerline of the valley.

4 Roofing Around Obstructions.
Adjust courses as you approach a vent stack or other obstruction so you can notch the shingles without cutting into the nailing bar. Courses can be adjusted up to 2 inches per course without becoming noticeable. Make sure each course has no more than a 9-inch exposure. Adjust the courses as you approach the ridge. The goal is to end up with full-depth panels. Before installing the last course, wrap a 10-inch-wide piece of felt over the ridge. Use standard precut ridge shingles to finish the job (see page 56).

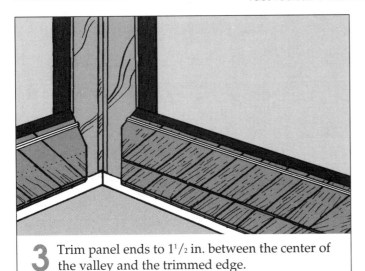

3 Trim panel ends to 1½ in. between the center of the valley and the trimmed edge.

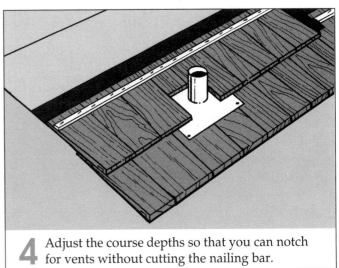

4 Adjust the course depths so that you can notch for vents without cutting the nailing bar.

Wood-Fiber Panels

Wood-fiber panels are another handy alternative to wood shingles. They are embossed with deep shadow lines and random-cut grooves that mimic the look of shakes. These 12x48-inch panels are applied lengthwise across the roof. They overlap with a shiplap joint between courses and a lap joint between shingles in the same course. The panels can be applied over solid sheathing or over old roofing (if the surface is sound and a layer of felt is added first). Cut the panels with a circular saw equipped with a plywood-cutting blade.

Wood-fiber panels are quick and easy to install and after a few months they weather to a silver-like gray that is very similar to cedar shingles. They can be used on roofs that have a 4 in 12 or greater pitch .

1 Applying the Starter Course.
Before installing wood-fiber shingles, apply a drip edge, 18 inch-wide, 30-pound felt at the eaves and 36 inch-wide, 30-pound felt underlayment. Cut 2½-inch-wide panel starter strips, applying them so that they overlap the eaves by 1 inch and the rakes by 2 inches. As you apply the the first course of full panels, offset the joints by 15 inches. Apply 8 fasteners per panel: Begin with one centered over the shiplap joint and end with one 3 inches in from the edge. Use 11-gauge roofing nails that penetrate 3/4 inch into the deck, or 16-gauge staples that penetrate 1 inch into the deck.

2 Applying Subsequent Courses.
Add the subsequent courses, offsetting end joints by at least 15 inches. The panels have two kinds of grooves in them: One type mimics the ridges found in a hand-split shake, the other type is deeper and mimics spaces between shingles. For appearance sake avoid lining up the deeper grooves even though functionally it makes no difference. Wood fiber panels have two score lines for your convenience: One for aligning the course, the other as a guide for nailing. Still, check the alignment every six or eight courses by measuring up from the eaves. Strike a chalk line if adjustment is needed.

3 Preparing the Valleys. Line the valleys with 36-inch felt and 24-inch wide W-metal. Trim panels to within a minimum of 4 inches from the centerline of the valley and clip 2 inches off the topmost corner of each panel along the valley

4 Finishing Ridges and Hips.
Ridges and hips are finished with manufactured caps that are scored with guidelines for spacing. After wrapping the ridge or hip with a 10-inch piece of felt, apply three fasteners in a triangular pattern to each shingle. Be careful to stay 1 inch inside of the overlap line.

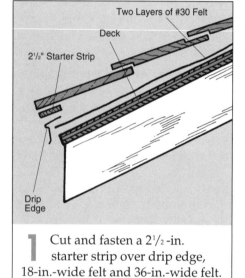

1 Cut and fasten a 2½-in. starter strip over drip edge, 18-in.-wide felt and 36-in.-wide felt.

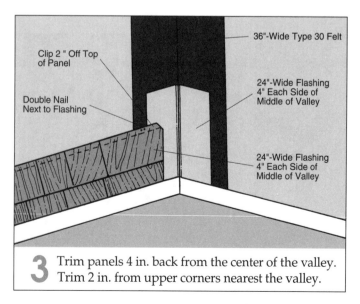

2 Stagger courses according to the pattern shown to achieve the best appearance and protection.

3 Trim panels 4 in. back from the center of the valley. Trim 2 in. from upper corners nearest the valley.

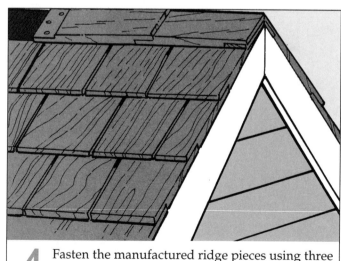

4 Fasten the manufactured ridge pieces using three nails 1 in. inside the overlap score line.

ROLL ROOFING & BUILT-UP ROOFING

Flat and low-pitch roofs require a roofing material that comes as close as possible to one single impermeable sheet. Roll roofing is a quick and easy solution. Built-up roofing also works, but the installation process is very involved and requires special equipment.

ROOFING CEMENT

Coping with Flat Roofs

Experience has proven that an absolutely flat roof leads to trouble. To avoid standing water which eventually causes leaks, a roof must have a minimum pitch of 1/4 inch per foot. If you are reroofing consider sheathing the roof to give it the minimal incline.

Roll roofing and built-up roofing are the most common techniques used to cover flat roofs. (Composition shingles are not used on roofs with a pitch of less than 2 in 12; wood shingles are not used on a pitch of less than 3 in 12; and shakes are not used on a pitch of less than 4 in 12.) Of the two methods, roll roofing is quicker and easier to handle. Built-up roofing requires special equipment that cannot readily be rented. It is included in this chapter only to facilitate hiring a professional to do the job.

Installing Roll Roofing

Roll roofing provides a quick, inexpensive roofing solution. Essentially made of the same material as composition shingles, roll roofing provides only one layer of covering as opposed to three layers. Compared to shingling, roll roofing is installed very quickly. A lot of territory is covered in a short time although it helps to have an assistant.

The life of roll roofing is typically 5 to 12 years. Given its plain appearance and short life, single-layer roll roofing is best used on sheds or in places where the roof is not visible. It may be used on slopes that are flatter than those normally covered by shingles, especially if a concealed nail application is used. Double-coverage selvage roll roofing is used for roofs that are nearly flat.

Roll roofing is more fragile than other roofing options. In temperatures below 45 degrees the material may crack. You can work in colder conditions if you warm the rolls first. The roofing

cement and lap cement must be kept at a temperature above 45 degrees, so store it indoors if you are working in cold weather.

Make sure the roofing has not curled at the edges or puckered in the middle. If it has, cut it into pieces 12 to 18 feet long and stack the pieces on a flat surface. Depending on the air temperature they will take an hour to one day to flatten.

Underlayment is not required, but since it is easy to install and so inexpensive, it is worth the extra effort. Install drip edge at the rakes and

eaves before roofing (see page 26). Even small pebbles and sticks eventually poke through roll roofing so sweep the surface with extra care.

Roll Roofing Option

An option to installing roll roofing horizontally to the rakes is to install it vertically. This eases the job when working on highly pitched roofs. Overlap pieces by 2 inches. Cement the seam and nail every 3 inches. Horizontal seams (where a new piece of roll roofing continues the vertical run) also must overlap 2 inches. Cement the seam and nail every 3 inches.

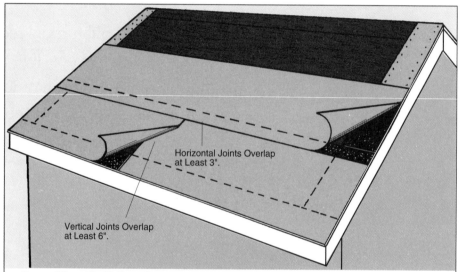

Horizontal Joints Overlap at Least 3".

Vertical Joints Overlap at Least 6".

Installing Roll Roofing. Applied with nails and roofing cement, roll roofing is a quick and inexpensive option.

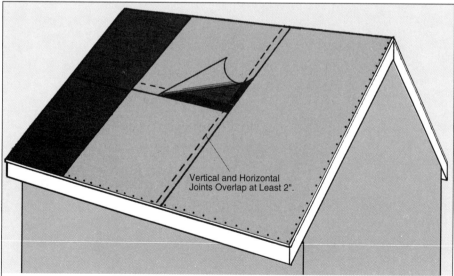

Vertical and Horizontal Joints Overlap at Least 2".

Roll Roofing Option. An alternative for a highly pitched roof is to apply roll roofing parallel to the rake.

Exposed Nail Method

The exposed nail method is the quickest and easiest way to install roll roofing.

1 Installing the First Course.

First protect each valley with an 18-inch-wide sheet, taking extra care to lay it completely flat. If the material is raised above the sheathing it will tear later if someone walks on it.

The eaves may be uneven so do not use it as a guide for aligning the first sheet. Instead snap a chalk line 35½ inches up from the eaves and run your first sheet so that it overhangs the eaves by 1/2 inch. Add 2 inches of roofing cement at eaves and nail all seams and edges every 3 inches Use galvanized roofing nails to penetrate the sheathing by at least 3/4 inch. Once you have "aimed" the sheet and put some nails down, you can't fix it if you find that it is headed off course. Avoid puckers and folds. Cut the course long enough so that some roofing overhangs the rake. When the roof is complete use a utility knife to trim the course flush with the edge of the drip edge. If you are reroofing and there is no drip edge, strike a line so the new roofing can be trimmed flush with the previous layer.

2 Nailing and Cementing. Snap
a chalk line 2 inches down from the top of the first sheet and carefully spread lap cement above this line.

3 Cutting and Nailing. Use the
roll of roofing itself as a guide to a straight, rough cut. Use the chalk line as a guide to nail down the next sheet. The lap cement seals all nails.

4 Covering Ridges and Hips.
Cover ridges and hips after you have roofed both sides. Cut a piece of roll roofing 12 inches wide, snap chalk lines down from the ridge on either side, apply lap cement above those lines and nail down the ridge sheet.

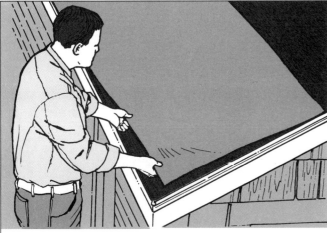

1 Position roll roofing along the eaves overlapping the edge by 1/2 in. Align to a chalk line snapped 35¹/₂ in. from the bottom edge.

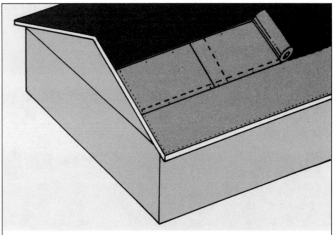

2 Strike a line 2 in. down from the top of the last course. Cement the seam, pressing down to ensure adhesion. Nail at 3 in. intervals.

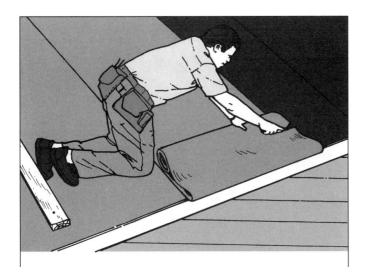

3 Roll to edge and then fold the roll back on itself. Use the roll as a cutting guide. Cut more roofing than needed and trim as a final step.

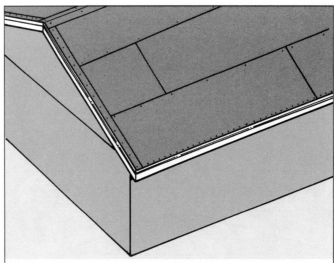

4 Cut a 12-in. piece of roll roofing. Snap chalk lines down from the ridge and apply lap cement above those lines. Nail down the ridge roofing.

Concealed Nail Method

The concealed nail method is ideal for low pitch roofs (1 in 12 or less) where slow-moving water might work its way under nailheads.

1 Adding Strips to Roof Edges. When installing a new roof begin by attaching 9-inch-wide starter strips of roll roofing along rakes and eaves. Use nails spaced 4 inches apart and 3/4 inch from the edge. These strips provide a surface to which the cement adheres.

2 Installing the First Course. Snap a chalk line 35½ inches from the eaves as a guide for rolling out the first course of roofing. This allows the 36-inch wide roll to over-hang the eaves by 1/2 inch. Attach the first course to the chalk line, nailing the top edges only. Nail every 4 inches, 3/4 inch from the top of the course. Trowel a rough 2-inch-wide layer of roofing cement under the first course at the eaves and the rake. Press down the seams to make sure they stick.

3 Installing Remaining Courses. Mark course overlaps as you go, by snapping a chalk line 6 inches down from the top of each course. Align the bottom of the next course and nail along the top edge only. Then go back and apply roofing cement at the rakes and at the over lap with the course below.

4 Covering Valleys. Begin by covering each valley with an 18-inch-wide sheet of roll roofing. Be careful to lay it completely flat. As courses of roll roofing are added onto roofs adjacent to the valley, let each run 12 inches past the valley. Cement (do not nail) seams within 6 inches of the center of the valley. Then add roofing to the opposite face of the roof, again letting it over-lap the valley. Trim down the center of the valley and cement into place.

5 Covering Ridges and Hips. Ridges and hips are covered after both sides are roofed. Cut a piece of roll roofing 12 inches wide, snap chalk lines 6 inches down. From the ridge on either side, apply lap cement above those lines, and seal down the ridge.

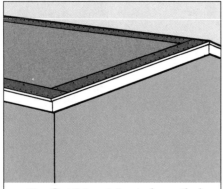

1 Cut 9 in. strips to be nailed 3/4 in. in from the edge at 4 in. intervals to the rakes and eaves of the roof.

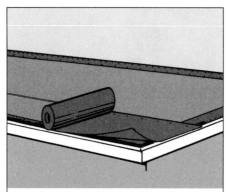

2 Strike a line 35½ in. from eaves edge as a guide for rolling out the roofing. Nail at top edge only.

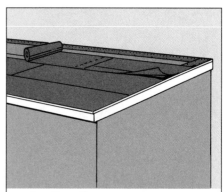

3 Install remaining courses overlapping them 6 in. Nail at top edges and cement course overlaps and rakes.

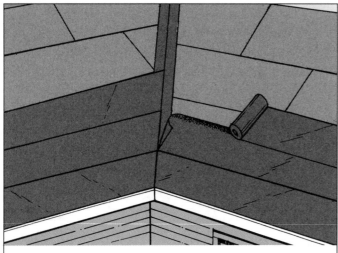

4 After roofing the valley, add the courses of roofing so that courses overlaps each other. Trim down the center of the valley.

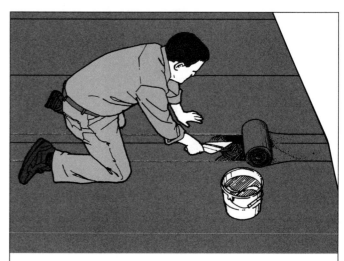

5 Cover the ridge with a 12-in. strip sealed in place with roofing cement.

Double Coverage Roll Roofing

Buy double coverage roll roofing (sometimes called selvage roofing) for those roofs that are nearly flat (up to 1 in 12). This material is applied with a 19-inch overlap called the selvage and 17-inch mineral-coated exposure. Selvage can be applied over shingle or roll roofing although it is best to remove old roofing, repair the sheathing and install drip edges. Each roll covers 51 square feet. Because of the thorough overlap it provides a double layer of roofing. Be sure to purchase the type that is applied with cold cement rather than hot asphalt.

1 Applying the Starter Strip. Double coverage roofing is applied directly to sheathing. Cut away the 17-inch mineral-coated section to be used as the starter strip. Use a broom-handled brush to apply a 17-inch-wide layer of roofing cement along the eaves. Then press the starter strip into the cement and roll it with a roofer's roller (these can be rented). Nail in two rows of nails at 12-inch intervals across the the surface.

2 Adding the Course. Position the first course over the starter strip. Nail it in place, with two horizontal rows of nails. Position the rows 4$\frac{1}{2}$ inches and 13 inches from the top of the course. Space nails in rows about 12 inches apart. Roll back the sheet and coat the selvage surface thickly with roofing cement.

3 Sealing Vertical Overlaps. Vertical seams are cemented rather than nailed and overlap by 6 inches. Nail the first sheet along the edge, spacing nails 4 inches apart and 1 inch in from the edge. Apply cement to the overlapping sheet, covering the first sheet 5$\frac{1}{2}$ inches in from its nailed edge. Nail the overlapping sheet in place (again nailing only on the selvage area). Press down the vertical seam for adhesion. Do not nail the exposed area.

1 Apply roofing cement along the eaves. Use the selvage section as a starter strip.

2 Nail selvage of first full course. Apply cement under mineral-coated exposure.

3 Overlap vertical seams by 6 in. Apply cement and seal. Nail the selvage area only.

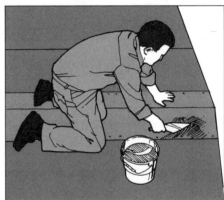

4 Seal hips and ridges with a selvage section starter and cement on next section.

4 Sealing Hips and Ridges. Finish hip and ridges by repeating the same procedure in miniature. Cut sections 12 inches wide from a roll of double coverage roofing (include both the selvage and exposed areas). Snap a line and apply a starter strip using only the selvage section of one piece. Nail the selvage section, spacing the nails at 4-inch intervals. Hammer one additional nail 1 inch in from the edge. Trowel on cement and add the next section as you would a shingle.

5 Trimming Rakes. As with roll roofing it is easiest to let the roofing overhang the rake and trim it when the roof is covered. Strike a line

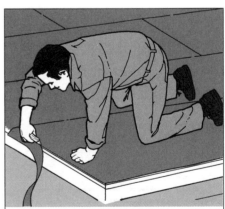

5 Snap a chalk line and use a utility knife to trim excess material at the rakes.

so that 1/4 inch of roofing overhangs the drip edge. Use a hook blade utility knife to trim the rake.

For extra protection use double layers of standard roll roofing. Cut a 19-inch strip as a starter course. Cement the starter strip to the deck and nail it every 12 inches. Overlap the starter course forming a 17-inch exposure. Apply roofing cement between layers and nail only the overlapped area. Overlap each course 6 inches vertically, cementing it and nailing every 2 inches where the next course will overlap.

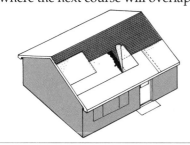

Built-Up Roofing

During the last 30 years many flat-roofed sections of homes, and in some cases whole homes, have been covered with a built-up roof (BUR). Do-it-yourselfers easily can patch built-up roofing (see page 16), but to install an entire built-up roof requires expensive specialized equipment. If you have a built-up roof and foresee major repairs or replacement, you will want to know the components of built-up roofs and how to judge the work of a professional crew.

Leaving it to the Professionals

Most built-up roofs are covered with three to five layers of heavy roofing felt coated with hot asphalt. A

Believed to be the most effective roofing for flat and low incline roofs, the installation of modified bitumen roofing is a job for professional roofers. Large sheets of roofing material are applied over layers of nailed felt. The material is lapped by 4 inches and usually sealed with a torch (hot tar or roofing cement is sometimes used). Unlike other roofing techniques that call for gravel, modified bitumen roofing is covered with aluminum paint.

Leaving it to the Professionals. Because of the need for applicators such as these, built-up roofing jobs are left to the professionals.

mineral surface of gravel or crushed rock often tops the job.

Depending on the number of layers applied and the way in which they are applied, a contractor guarantees the work for 10 to 20 years. If you hire a professional make sure that a guarantee is in the contract.

Tools used by contractors range from simple mops and buckets to high-cost spraying equipment. The

best job requires hot roofing in which the asphalt coating is heated in large kettles before being applied. Built-up roofing is thick but by no means indestructible. When a roof begins to split or develops deep alligatoring (checked cracks that resemble alligator skin) it is time to have it inspected.

If serious alligatoring appears within a year or so of installation, the hot asphalt probably was laid too thickly and the job needs to be redone. Sometimes within several years of installation the roofing comes apart from the roof below or pulls away from other surfaces such as adjoining walls (this is called delaminating). These problems are caused when the surface of the roof is not completely cleared of debris or water before installation. If alligatoring or delaminating occurs, the roof must be redone.

Flashing Built-Up Roofs. The greatest potential for trouble is found in the places where the roof deck meets a vertical wall. A cant strip is placed in such a corner to soften the angle between roof and wall and to keep water from standing in the joint. Tile or metal flashing ideally overlaps the roofed surface.

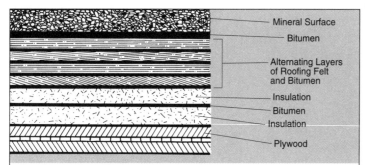

Built-up Roofing. As its name implies, built-up roofing consists of several layers beginning with plywood sheathing.

Mineral Surface
Bitumen
Alternating Layers of Roofing Felt and Bitumen
Insulation
Bitumen
Insulation
Plywood

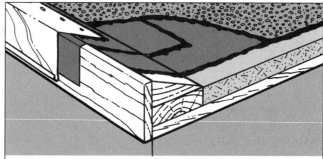

Flashing Built-up Roofs. Beveled strips of wood and a layer of flashing protects vulnerable joints.

OTHER ROOFING OPTIONS

Slate, tile, metal, and fiberglass are attractive roofing alternatives. All options are worth considering, although some are expensive and others require specific expertise. Whether you do the job yourself or decide to hire a professional, learning about these roofing materials and their installation can save you money and ensure better results.

Slate Roofing

Slate is the most expensive roofing option; even its very long life (from 50 to 100 years) hardly makes it financially practical. But nothing else provides the rugged-yet-classy look of slate. Slate can be placed over a layer of composition shingles only if the pitch of the roof is 4 in 12 or more and only if a structural engineer has confirmed the roof framing can bear slate's 7-pounds-per-square-foot weight. If you are an experienced do-it-yourselfer who is willing to embark on a major project, you might consider buying slating tools and learning the craft. However, slating is a skill that demands considerable investment—an investment better put toward the cost of hiring a professional.

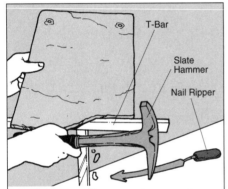

Slate Roofing. Applying a slate roof requires three specialized tools: A nail ripper, a hammer equipped with a sharp edge and a point, and a T-bar for trimming.

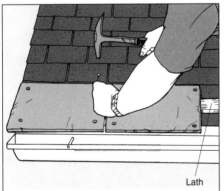

Shimming the Starter Course. A piece of lath is nailed to the roof under the starter course. This gives the first course an upward tilt at the eaves.

Slate is simply unprocessed stone that has been mined from the ground and cut to size. It is available in a wide variety of grades and thicknesses, so ask a salesman how long your selection is expected to last. Slate comes in many colors from gray to shades of green, purple and red. Some colors fade after years of exposure. Slate also can be smooth or rough surfaced. Different colors and textures may be used on a single roof, but be wary of this; you may not like the patterns that emerge.

Slate is heavy. Just how heavy depends on the grade. Be sure your roof can handle the load. Many local codes require specific reinforcements if you want to put slate over an existing roof. Copper flashing is recommended because it is long-lasting and looks good with slate.

The professionals use three simple, but specialized tools: a nail ripper, which is used to cut off a nail level to the surface; a hammer equipped with a sharp edge for cutting slate and a point for poking nailholes in the slate, and a T-bar which aids in trimming.

Fiber-Cement Roofing. If you love the look of slate but you do not have the money to put into it, you can use a compromise material. New varieties of slate-like fiber-cement roofing are light, attractive and warranted for 40 years. These new products not only look a lot like slate, but they also share much of its durability and are worth investigating. Like slate, they are typically contractor installed.

Installing Slate

The following list outlines the basic procedures used for installing a slate roof.

Shimming the Starter Course. Slate tilts slightly upward at the eaves, extending 1/2 inch beyond the rake and 1 inch beyond the eaves. Use a piece of lath to shim the starter course which is made up of slates set lengthwise.

Installing Felt Underlayment. Slate often is laid on one layer of 30-pound roofing felt. Some contractors prefer to use individual felt strips under each course to provide additional cushioning.

Installing the Slates. Two nails, installed in pre-punched holes, hold each slate. The slates are set so their beveled edges show. There is a 1/16-inch gap between slates.

Offsetting the Gaps. The gaps between slates are offset by at least 2 inches.

Installing Felt Underlayment. Slates are cushioned by felt underlayment between courses.

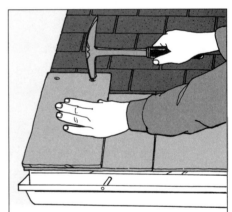

Installing the Slates. Each slate is held in place by two nails in pre-punched holes.

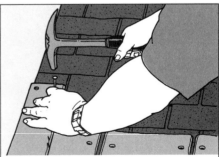

Offsetting the Gaps. An offset of at least 2 in. is used between gaps between slates.

Capping the Ridge. All of the slates at the ridge are the same width. The peak overlap is alternated from one side of the roof to the other.

Capping the Ridge. The ridge is capped with slates that are the same width. The overlap at the peak is alternated from one side of the roof to the other. Slates are fastened to the ridge with two nails.

Working with Slate

■ Use solid copper- or zinc-coated nails. These are nailed through factory-punched holes in each slate.

■ Give slate roofs extra pitch (called canting) at the eaves. Before slating, a 1/4-inch-thick strip of wood is nailed along the eaves. This causes the bottom course of slate to turn upwards slightly. It also gives the roof a classic appearance and provides additional drip protection for the fascia.

■ To prevent cracking the slate courses use proper scaffolding (or make sure your contractor uses proper scaffolding).

■ Slate nails do not penetrate metal flashing. Unlike the nails used with shingle roofs, these nails have no way of sealing themselves.

■ Use plenty of roofing cement under hip and ridge slates. All exposed nailheads also must be covered with cement.

■ Slates must lap over the underlying course by at least 3 inches.

■ Slates with hairline cracks are discarded; cracks only worsen over time.

Maintaining & Repairing Slate

There is little maintenance involved when it comes to a slate roof. The only thing you have to worry about is debris that traps moisture along eaves and degrades the slate. Broken slates can be replaced, but you will need a slate ripper to remove the damaged portion.

1 Clipping Nails. Slip the nail under the slate to be replaced. Hook the ripper onto the shaft of a nail that holds the slate in place. Hammer the ripper to cut the nail. Repeat with the second nail to release the slate.

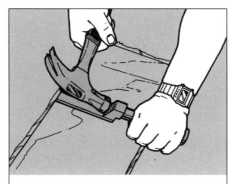

1 Hammer the nail ripper to cut the nails holding a damaged shingle.

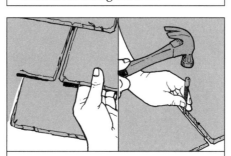

2 To cut slate, punch a series of holes on the back of the slate then sever along the line.

4 Replace the slate and use a nail set to drive galvanized nails flush with the slate surface.

2 Cutting a Replacement. Cut slate to size with a carborundum circular saw blade. You also can use a nail set to punch a series of holes along the cut line, and then holding the cut line even with the edge of a bench or other hard edge, crack off the excess. Wear goggles.

3 Marking Nailholes. Slip a new slate into the space and mark for nailholes in the crack between shingles in the overlapping course. If two cracks overlap the replacement shingle make a mark at both. Then remove the slate and use a 1/8-inch masonry bit to drill holes.

4 Nailing the Gap. Put back the slate and use a nail set to gently drive an 8d galvanized finishing nail flush with the slate surface.

5 Covering the Nailhead. Use two screwdrivers to gently pry the overlapping slates. Cut a piece of copper roughly 5x6 inches and bend it until it is slightly cupped. Slip the cupped copper sheet over the nailhead to seal it. Friction holds the the sheet in place.

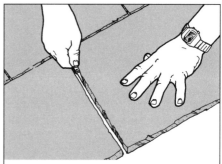

3 Position the replacement slate and mark holes for nailing between the overlapping shingles.

5 Gently pry up overlapping shingles and slip in a cupped piece of copper over nailhole.

Tile Roofing

Like slate, classic glazed clay tiles last from 50 to 100 years and possess a timeless quality few other materials have to offer. Tiles also are expensive and very heavy, weighing as much as 1000 pounds to the square. Concrete tiles are a smart substitute. They look good, last almost as long as glazed tiles, and are light enough to be installed on some standard roofs intended for composition shingles.

If you are considering a tile or concrete tile roof consult your roofing supply source and local building department to make sure your roof can handle the tiles you choose. Do not tile over a roof that has a slope flatter than 3 in 12.

Although more difficult to apply than shingles, tiles can be installed by a skilled do-it-yourselfer. In addition to the tools used for installing composition shingles, you also will need a circular saw with a masonry-cutting blade.

Caution: *Wear protective goggles when cutting tiles.*

If you can fit it into your budget, use copper nails rather than galvanized nails. An advantage to using copper nails is that they are soft enough to cut through should you have to replace a tile. Copper nails also allow enough give so that if you nail them too far into the tiles, the tiles will not crack as the decking moves with temperature variations. Hammer all nails, no matter what kind, to within a nickel's thickness of the tile surface.

Preparing the Deck

Although there are various ways to install tile, a few basics prevail. Your tiles will come with instructions pertaining to whether or not they require underlayment. Some tiles are nailed directly to sheathing, while others require battens to be laid first. Battens are 1x2 strips of redwood or pressure-treated pine that are spaced at intervals that match the tile exposure (14 inches is typical). Further preparations also may be called for, such as one 2x2 along all ridges and hips, 1x2 starter strips along eaves and rakes, or 1x3 nailed to rake rafters to allow the tiles to extend further sideways. Check manufacturer's instructions.

Use flashing that will last as long as your tiles. Copper is best. Apply metal drip edge along the eaves before the underlayment (if any) is installed. Along the rakes, the drip edge is installed after the underlayment. Take special care in the valleys; first put down 90-pound mineral-surfaced roll roofing, then W-metal that is at least 24 inches wide (see page 25). Cover hips and ridges with a double layer of felt.

Tile Alternatives. Tiles are designed to interlock so the amount of exposure is always readily apparent. Nail them down to the sheathing or "hang" them on the battens. If your roof has a pitch of 7 in 12 or steeper, or if you live in an area subject to high winds, fasten every third or fourth course with metal clips.

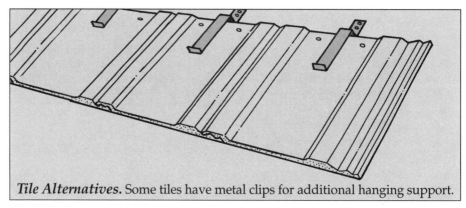

Tile Alternatives. Some tiles have metal clips for additional hanging support.

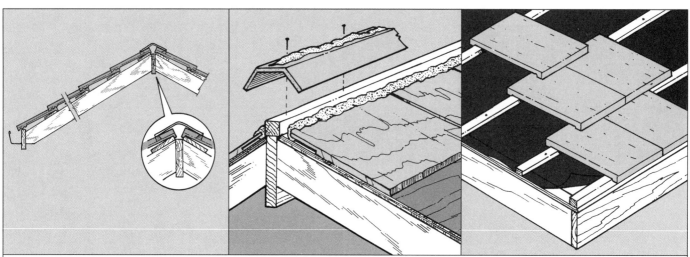

Preparing the Deck. Tiles are attached to battens and interlock between courses (left). Some tiles can be directly attached to roof sheathing. The ridge is sealed with mortar and a cap (center). Concrete tiles lock onto 1x2 battens attached to the decking (right).

1. *Setting the Tile Width*. The positioning of the tiles is crucial (you cannot end at a rake with half a tile). Snap a chalk line as a guide along the eaves. Tiles hang over the eaves by 2 inches. Nail the gable rake tiles in place, overlapping the drip edge. By dividing the total length of the eaves by the width of a tile, determine the distance each tile will be set apart and mark the drip edge accordingly. Tiles provide about 1 inch of sideways leeway where they overlap the previous tile. Set the eaves closure tiles flush with the eaves edge and nail in place.

2. *Setting the Tile*. Apply roofing mastic where one tile overlaps the other. Set the first tile in place and nail with a 6d nail.

3. *Nailing the First Course*. Install six tiles using the marks along the rake and the horizontal chalk line as positioning guides. Double-check your width calculation to make sure the course ends with a full-width tile.

4. *Adding the second course*. Work up the roof in stair-step fashion. Overlap the tiles by at least 3 inches.

5. *Finishing the Course*. Lay the left-hand rake tiles. Toenail a 1x3 nailer that runs from eaves to ridge. Position it so that it lines up with holes in the tile that are provided for nailing. Nail the last tile of each course to this nailer.

6. *Laying the Ridge*. Lay a bed of tinted mortar and set ridge starter tiles. Apply the hip and ridge tiles over the ridge, overlapping each by at least 3 inches.

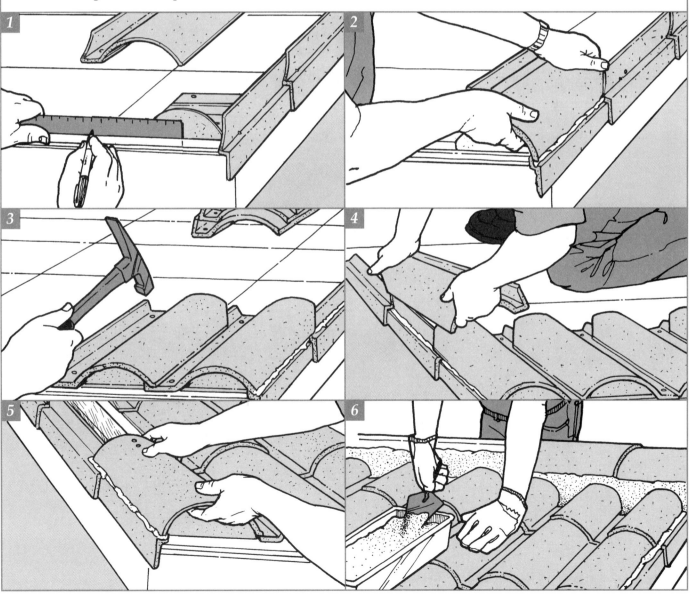

Before committing to a contractor, check his/her references and make sure he/she is certified to install the material you have chosen. Visit nearby sites and use the following tips to help evaluate the contractor:

Use of Sealant. Tape sealant is used within joints, but almost never on the surface where it can be seen (and where it can wear off with time). Too much reliance on sealant might be a sign that the contractor is not installing the material correctly. Expect some visible sealant in places where ridge panels join and around the vent stack sleeves.

Signs of Quality Work. Check that panels are straight, and that details at the rakes and eaves are neat. Denting, particularly in the valley, is a sign of poor craftsmanship. Check that stack penetrations are neat and that minimal sealant is used on them.

Check for Other Metals. Lead stack sleeves, steel antenna wires, and copper gutters all contain a metal that corrodes the roofing. An experienced contractor knows to replace these problem items.

Few Exposed Fasteners. The standing seam system has exposed fasteners only on the rake and eaves trim, and then only sparingly. If exposed fasteners are used they must be coated, long-life fasteners.

Get the Manual. Manufacturers want their systems to be applied correctly and most will not hesitate to send you a manual. Use it as a guide to asking the right questions.

Metal Roofing

The metal roof is experiencing new popularity. This may be due to the success of metal roofs on commercial buildings, or perhaps the historical appropriateness of metal roofing on older homes. Metal boasts a longevity surpassed only by slate and tile—at a considerably lower cost.

Standing-seam panel roofing is the most common type of metal roofing for residential use. These panels, which run vertically, usually are made of aluminum or galvanized steel, but in some cases they are made of zinc and aluminum-coated steel. Since the panels are painted, they offer more color options than other types of roofing. Metal roofing is ideal for restoring older homes that originally had metal roofs.

This light material (one pound per square foot) is suitable for covering old roofs and may even be used over three layers of composition shingles (if local codes permit). For roofs that have irregularities, narrow, textured and dull-finish panels are best.

The metal roofing shown here can cover a roof with a pitch of at least 3 in 12. Other metal roof systems handle roofs with pitches as slight as 1/4-inch in 12 (usually a job for built-up roofing). However, the experience and special equipment of a contractor is needed for its installation.

The installation process involves laying 12 to 16 1/2-inch panels and correctly joining them at the seams, wall flashing, valleys and ridges. The panels are precut to the exact length ordered up to 40 feet long (for this reason horizontal seams are very

Metal Roofing. Metal roofing requires some special tools and experience to install.

unlikely on most homes). Metal roofing can be applied to plywood decking with an underlayment of 30-pound felt. Laying and joining the panels is not difficult, but handling eaves edges, rakes, wall flashing valleys and ridges requires experience.

Installing Metal Roofing

As mentioned, installing metal roofing requires some special tools and experience. Here's an overview of what is involved.

Installing Felt and Eaves Trim.
Thirty-pound felt provides a moisture barrier over plywood decking. Metal roofing is applied vertically, completing a 12- to 16½-inch panel from eaves to ridge before applying the next. Check the squareness of the roof and adjust for irregularity. Eaves trim is screwed in place and sealant is applied to the edge before panels are clipped in place.

Applying the First Rake Edge.
After the first vertical panel has been set, the first rake edge (applied on either side of the roof depending on the installer's preference) is applied over the panel. Underlayment overlaps the rake edge.

Joining the Panels.
Clips and sealant join the panels. Clips are applied every 12 inches where high winds prevail, every 18 inches elsewhere. No adhesive is necessary to seal the sheets to the decking. Do not step on the seams. In fact, walk on the sheets as little as possible. Scratched finishes may void the warranty.

Installing Valley Flashing.
Valley flashing is set on a piece of 30-pound felt underlayment that lines the valley. Channels running parallel in the valley are sealed and screwed to it and hold the edge of the panels.

Sealing Ridge Flashing.
At the ridges, flashing is sealed to "Z" strips that are fastened between the standing seams.

Installing Felt and Eaves Trim. Trim is installed and sealed before panels are installed.

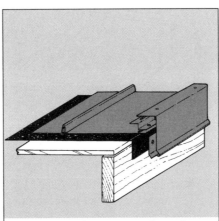

Applying the First Rake Edge. The first rake edge is appled after the first vertical panel has been set.

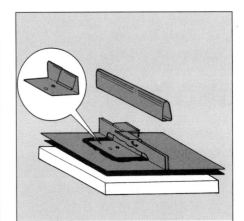

Joining the Panels. Clips and sealant join the panels. No adhesive is needed to seal the sheets.

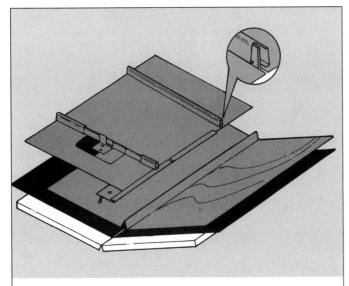

Installing Valley Flashing. Channels running parallel in a valley are sealed and screwed in.

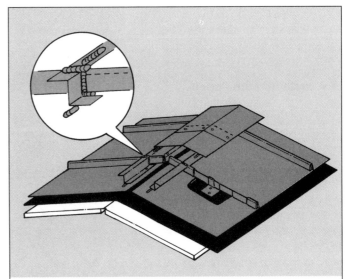

Sealing Ridge Flashing. At the ridges, flashing is sealed to "Z" strips that are fastened between the seams.

Panel Roofing

Corrugated panel roofs made of fiberglass provide a watertight, yet translucent covering for decks, carports, and greenhouses. In addition, corrugated aluminum and galvanized metal panels are easy to install and are long-lasting solutions for utility buildings. Panels of both types typically are sold along with manufacturer-specific nails, filler strips and caulk. Install according to manufacturer's instructions.

Panel roofing is a quick and easy roofing solution, but keep in mind that fiberglass easily chips and metal tends to dent and bend—both are problems that cannot be fixed. The panels expand and contract with temperature changes and if not installed correctly this causes the roof to come detached. In addition to the roofing material, the job requires filler strips (pieces of wood shaped to fit the contours of the panels) and special nails (aluminum for aluminum roofs, steel for steel roofs) fitted with plastic washers.

1 **Framing the Panel.** Install 1x4 framing set on two-by rafters in accordance with local municipal codes. In areas of heavy snow, slope must be at least 8 in 12. No underlayment or drip edge is required. Panels also can be added over old roofing by applying 1x4 nailers every 2 to 4 feet. Use nails that penetrate the sheathing by at least 3/4 inch.

2 **Installing the Panels.** In places where a complete seal against the weather is necessary, place filler strips under the roofing at the eaves. The strips are shaped to conform to the profile of the panels. Install the filler strips as you work your way across the the roof, beginning with the first full-width panel. Panels typically are 26 inches wide. Nail four nails across the panel where it rests on a framing piece. When working with steel and fiberglass, predrill a hole for each nail. Nail carefully so the

roofing is snug to the framing but not indented. Overlap panels 1 inch lengthwise. Lay a bead of adhesive caulk across the length of each seam where panels overlap. For translucent fiberglass panels use clear silicone caulk. Panels are available in lengths up to 20 feet. If you need more than one panel from eaves to ridge, overlap by 12 inches on slopes greater than 4 in 12; 18 inches on lower slopes.

3 **Installing Ridge Cap.** Install ridge cap at ridges and hips. Some styles require filler strips, while others are shaped to fit the roofing. Nail at ridges according to the manufacturer's recommended pattern. Do not nail edges that will be overlapped. Overlap panels with the ridge cap by at least an inch. Overlap sections of ridge panel by 6 inches.

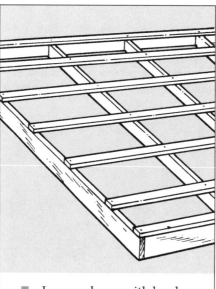

1 In accordance with local codes, construct framing out of 1x4s.

2 Allow panels to overhang rake by 1/4 to 3/8 in., and eaves by 2 in. Overlap panels side-by-side 1 in.

3 Install ridge cap at ridges and hips. Some styles require filler strips while others are shaped to fit the roofing. Overlap panels with the ridge cap by 1 in.

REPAIRING & MAINTAINING RAIN GUTTERS

Gutters and downspouts are your home's second line of defense when it comes to the battle against the elements. Not only do gutters carry off water from the roof, they also play a key part in protecting the structure of your home. Time spent maintaining gutters pays off in peace of mind.

Re-inventing the Gutter

Materials used for North American gutters have evolved from wooden troughs to galvanized steel to aluminum. Vinyl, the latest material, may be the best yet. It combines its ease of maintenance with greater resistance to impact. Along with snap-together installation, it also is the ideal material for do-it-yourselfers. Copper gutters, although beautiful and long-lasting, are very costly.

Aluminum. This metal is durable, noncorrosive, and quite strong for its light weight. Suppliers offer a standard grade (.027 gauge) and a premium grade (.032 gauge). Both are available in a wide range of coordinating colors. The premium grade may be ordered from specialty dealers in lengths up to 32 feet. Heavier gauges resist damage from ladders and impact. The cost of a premium-grade aluminum system may equal or exceed the cost of a vinyl system.

Vinyl. This plastic is more resistant to impact and easier to install than aluminum. Vinyl systems offer options such as high-flow drop outlets and attachments that eject leaves and debris. A high-flow outlet increases capacity 150 percent or more without increasing gutter or downspout diameter. Leaf separators and molded-in ribs on gutter floors allow the rainwater to flush the system and eject leaves, minimizing annual gutter maintenance.

Parts of a Gutter & Downspout

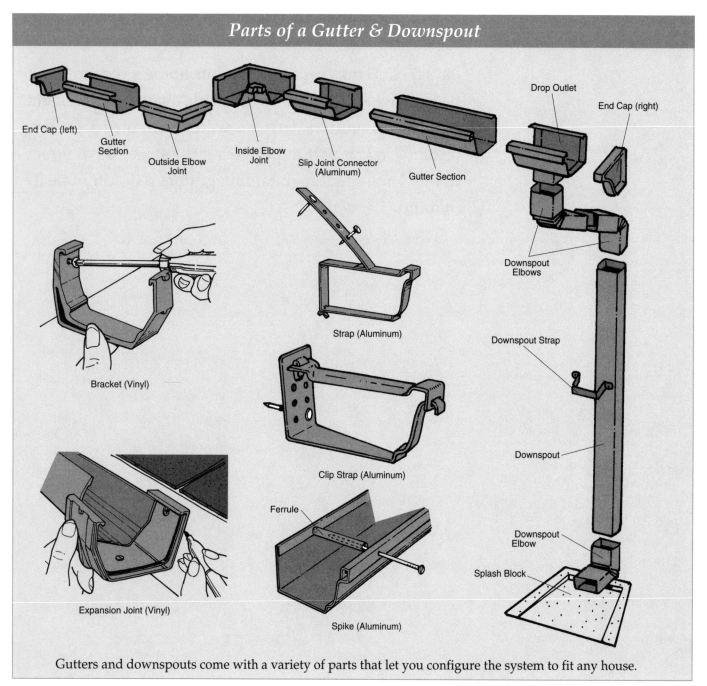

End Cap (left)
Gutter Section
Outside Elbow Joint
Inside Elbow Joint
Slip Joint Connector (Aluminum)
Gutter Section
Drop Outlet
End Cap (right)
Downspout Elbows
Bracket (Vinyl)
Strap (Aluminum)
Downspout Strap
Clip Strap (Aluminum)
Downspout
Ferrule
Expansion Joint (Vinyl)
Spike (Aluminum)
Downspout Elbow
Splash Block

Gutters and downspouts come with a variety of parts that let you configure the system to fit any house.

Repairing Gutters

If gutters are badly broken or rusted, it is time to replace them. Many problems, however, can be repaired.

Replacing Damaged Hangers.
Sagging gutters often are the result of a broken strap hanger. A simple machine screw, washer, and nut replace the loose rivet. If the strap is severed, replace it or use a pop riveter to splice in a new hanger. If necessary, strike a plumb from one end of the section to the other as a guide for realigning the hanger.

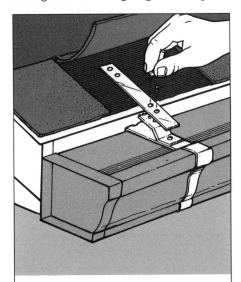

Replacing Damaged Hangers. Renew a worn strap by splinting on a new aluminum strap.

Adjusting Slope. Quickly fix a sagging gutter by crimping the strap hangers to true up the slope.

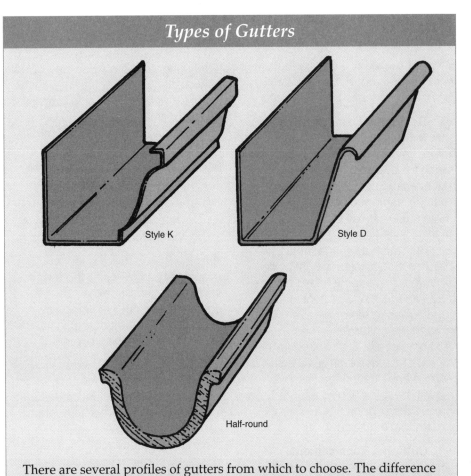

Types of Gutters

Style K

Style D

Half-round

There are several profiles of gutters from which to choose. The difference is almost completely aesthetic. Wood gutters are the most expensive and require the highest maintenance.

Adjusting Slope. A slight dip or sag in a gutter causes runoff to pool and cascade down the wall. Adjust the strap of a sagging gutter by lifting up on the gutter while using pliers to bend a slight kink into the strap. Spikes and ferrules must be removed, the pitch of the gutter corrected, and additional hangers added.

Patching Holes. A metal gutter is patched with an epoxy body filler kit (available at automotive or hardware stores). Remove dirt and patches of rust or corrosion around the hole. Wipe the surface thoroughly with a rag dipped in paint thinner. When the area is dry, cut a piece of fiberglass cloth 1 inch larger than the hole. Mix a small amount of epoxy and use a putty knife to apply a layer around the hole. Press the fiberglass cloth into the epoxy. Then smooth the epoxy over the patch, filling and saturating the cloth.

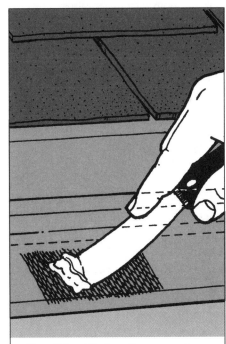

Patching Holes. Epoxy and mesh from an auto-body patch kit adds life to a rusted-out gutter.

Replacing a Section of Metal Gutter

Even if a section of the gutter becomes worn beyond repair, it does not mean the entire gutter has to be replaced.

1 Removing Damaged Section. Mark the incline of the old gutter before you remove it. (A gutter slopes 1 inch for every 20 feet of length.) If necessary, detach the downspout from the damaged section. Use an angle square to lay out a square cut on the section that needs to be removed. Attach a rope to the damaged section as support until it can be lowered. Wedge a board between gutter and fascia to protect the roof edge. Wearing safety goggles, cut through the gutter with a hacksaw. (A short piece of 2x4 slipped inside the rim of gutter minimizes the saw's binding and chattering.) Finish the cut with tin snips (if necessary). Then remove the supports and lower the section to the ground.

2 Cutting a Replacement. Determine the number of drop outlets, caps, corners and hangers needed. Measure the length of gutter replacement needed. Gutter sections can be joined with slip joints which are available at hardware stores. Slip joints are easy to install, but they must be supported by a nearby hanger (no more than 18 inches away). Wearing safety goggles, use a hacksaw to cut new sections to length (or use tin snips to minimize chipping prepainted gutter stock). Smooth the burrs from the cut edges with a flat metal file. Use sealant to preassemble the pieces on the ground. Connect end caps, corners, and drop outlets.

3 Joining New and Old. You can use a slip joint, lap joint or rivets to join the gutter pieces.

■ Apply mastic to the gutter and attach a slip joint. Install the section, apply more mastic to the joint and press the sections firmly together. Bend the rear tip of the slip joint, inward and crimp it with pliers.

■ To use a lap joint, slide the length of gutter farthest from the drop outlet into the nearer length until there is a 6-inch overlap. If necessary, trim back some of the inside gutter lip to allow full overlap. Then slide the joint apart and apply a 6-inch band of sealant to the bottom of the outside gutter length. Slip sections together and press down to seal.

■ To join the gutters with rivets, overlap by 2 inches and apply sealant as described. Use a pop riveter to drill and rivet the bottom and each side of the overlap. Dab each rivet head with sealant (otherwise pop rivets are not quite watertight). Reuse hangers to support the replacement section.

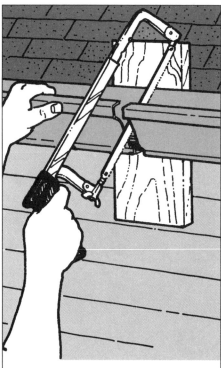

1 Protect the drip edge and eaves with a scrap of wood before using a hacksaw to cut off the damaged section.

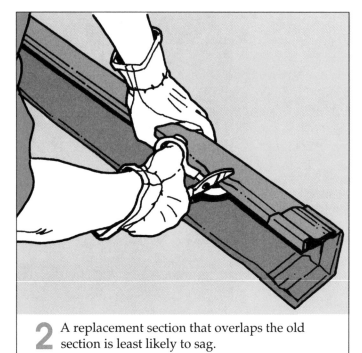

2 A replacement section that overlaps the old section is least likely to sag.

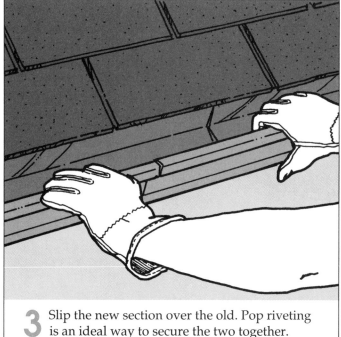

3 Slip the new section over the old. Pop riveting is an ideal way to secure the two together.

Replacing a Section of Vinyl Gutter

1 Removing Damaged Section. Vinyl expands and contracts with temperature changes. Vinyl gutter sections are joined with slip joints, which are designed to allow for movement caused by temperature changes. They also double for hangers. The easiest way to make a repair is to replace a section between two slip joints. Simply twist and pull the damaged section out of the slip joint.

2 Cut Replacement Gutter to Length. If the gutter you are replacing is in one piece, you can measure it to determine the length of the replacement. Otherwise, you will find a mark in each bracket to show how far the gutter is inserted into the joints. Measure between these marks to determine the length of the replacement gutter. Cut a new section to the proper length. Use a rounded metal file to smooth the cut edges. Then preassemble as much as possible on the ground. Connect end caps and drop outlets.

3 Preparing the Joint. Position the slip joint hanger at the point where the section was removed. Lubricate the gasket seals so the new section is able to move as it expands and contracts.

4 Installing New Section. To install the new section, tip the back edge of the gutter into the brackets and rock the piece toward you. Slide it into the expansion joint.

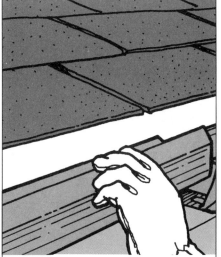

1 Twist and pull the damaged section out of the slip joint. Be careful not to damage hangers.

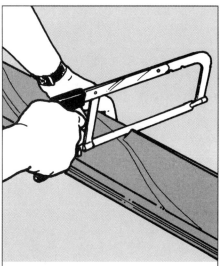

2 Measure a replacement section and cut it to length. Smooth the edges with a metal file.

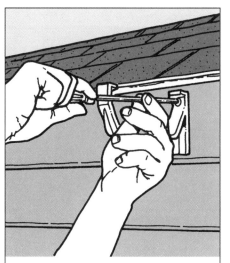

3 Before installing the replacement piece replace damaged hangers. Attach them at rafter ends.

4 Rotate the gutter down and rearward, until the front rim of the fitting snaps over the gutter.

Designing a New System

Before replacing the gutters evaluate the effectiveness of your present system. Can it cope with the occasional cloudburst or does it often overflow? Does the corner downspout spill a sheet of water across the driveway? These are signs that your gutter system needs redesigning.

A rule of thumb to remember: Four-inch gutters handle runoff from 750 square feet of roof; 5-inch gutters handle up to 1500 square feet; and more than 1500-square feet of roof requires 6-inch gutters.

Making a Sketch

Make a sketch of the new system on paper and include all dimensions. Add a drop outlet for every 35 to 40 feet of run.

Plan the number of drop outlets, inside and outside corners, slip joints, downspout sections, elbows (three per downspout) and straps (two per 8-foot section). Indicate a support hanger every 24 to 32 inches and at each end of gutter corners.

Tack a nail into the fascia 1½ inches below the roof edge at the high point of the gutter slope. Measure the length of run and calculate the correct amount of fall with a ratio of 1 inch in 20 feet. At the opposite end add the fall to 1½ inches and snap a chalk line at this slope.

Maintaining the Gutters

Unclogging a Downspout. Remove as much debris as possible from inside the drop outlet. Use a garden hose to flush the remaining blockage through the elbows. If it remains blocked, push the garden hose or a plumber's snake into the downspout. If blockage persists, remove the splash block elbow and try working from below. When the downspout is clear use a garden hose to flush it from above. Equip the gutter with a leaf strainer or full-coverage gutter screens to prevent future clogging.

Flushing a Gutter. Starting at the high end of the gutter run, and working toward the downspout, remove accumulated leaves and debris from the gutter, roof edge and valleys. With a garden hose and whisk broom or putty knife, brush and flush out remaining dirt and debris.

Managing Runoff To avoid basement seepage and foundation damage (plus erosion and saturated planting beds) water is directed away from the house. Some local codes forbid direct connection, to storm sewers, so that leaves you with three options for runoff: splash blocks, subsurface drain lines and dry wells. The quickest solution (and one that may immediately correct wet basement problems) is the installation of simple splash blocks sloped to carry water away from the foundation. In places where the grade is not sloped, connect downspouts to a plastic drain tile trenched in the soil. This corrugated, flexible pipe has serrations that allow drainage into the gravel bed. Pitch the trench away from the house.

A dry well is a pit dug at least 10 feet from the house at the end of a drain tile line. It is about 4 feet in diameter and 4 feet deep. Line the sides with landscape weed barrier and fill it with stone. Then cover with weed barrier (to prevent silting) and lay sod over the top.

Unclogging a Downspout. Clean clogged downspouts with a plumber's snake.

Flushing a Gutter. Use a garden hose and a whisk broom to flush debris from the gutter.

Managing Runoff. A downspout extension and splash blocks is the simplest method of carrying runoff away from the house (left). A buried drain line is perforated to distribute runoff underground (center). A dry well is at least 6 ft. deep and filled with loose rock and rubble (right).

Alignment notch A cutout projection or slit on the ends or sides of shingles that acts as a guide in application to secure a proper exposure.

Asphalt A bituminous compound, dark brown or black in color, used in the manufacture of asphalt roofing shingles.

Blind nailing Nails driven so that the heads are concealed.

Built-up roofing An outer covering of a comparatively flat roof, consisting of several layers of saturated and/or saturated-and-coated felt, each layer mopped with hot tar or asphalt as laid. The top layer is finished with a mineral or rock covering or with a special coating.

Butt That portion of a shingle exposed to the weather, also called the tab of the shingle.

Closed valley A valley in which the roofing material is laced or woven through the valley intersection.

Collars or vent sleeves Sheet-metal-flanged collars placed around vent pipes to seal the roofing around the vent pipe openings.

Counter flashing Strips of metal, roofing or fabric inserted so as to shed water onto the base flashing.

Course Horizontal unit of shingles running the length of the roof.

Cricket A small peaked saddle built behind the chimney or over an entry. It's purpose is to divert water to either side.

Cutout Slot or notch in a shingle that makes tabs look like individual shingles.

Deck The structural skin of a roof over which roofing is applied. Most homes built within the last 40 years use plywood for this purpose. (See Sheathing.)

Double coverage A method of applying roof shingles that provides two complete layers of protection.

Drip course First course of shingles at the eaves.

Eaves Edge of roof that projects over the outside wall.

Exposure Portion of shingle exposed to the weather, measured from butt of one shingle to butt of next course.

Fascia Horizontal trim at eaves that covers the rafter ends.

Flashing Material used to prevent seepage of water around any intersection or projection in a roof, including vent pipes, chimneys, adjoining walls, dormers and valleys.

Gable The triangular area of exterior wall of a building .

Hip The line of intersection of two sloping roof planes with walls that are not parallel to each other.

Hip roof A roof which rises from all four sides of a building.

Lacing or Weaving Interweaving of a course of shingles at an intersection of a roof; e.g., at 90-degree angles in a valley.

Laid to the weather (See Exposure)

Lap To overlap the surface of one shingle or other type of roofing material with another; also the length of such an overlap.

Lean-to roof Has one slope only and is built against a higher wall.

Open valley Type of valley on a roof in which roofing material is trimmed and flashing is exposed.

Ridge The horizontal line at which two roof planes meet when both roof planes slope down from that line.

Roll Roofing Roofing laid from a roll of material.

Roofer's cement A quick-setting asphalt adhesive for use with roofing materials.

Run The horizontal distance from the eaves to a point directly under the ridge of a roof.

Pitch Height from the joist to the ridge, divided by the rafter length; this equates to rise in inches per horizontal foot.

Rake A slope or inclination of a roof; the same as the slope.

Run wild To leave a piece of roofing or other material untrimmed until fastened.

Seal down An asphalt adhesive factory applied so that the shingles, once installed, have a concealed strip of sealing compound that securely bonds each shingle to provide wind resistance.

Sheathing The wooden foundation of a roof, also known as the deck. Typically made of 1/2-inch construction-grade plywood, older homes may have shiplap or planks.

Slope The degree of inclination of a roof plane in inches of rise per horizontal foot.

Soffit The finished underside of an eaves.

Soil stacks (See Vents)

Span The horizontal measurement from eaves to eaves.

Square An area of exposed roofing 10 feet square or comprising 100 square feet.

Square butt shingles Strip shingles that usually have two or three tabs formed by cutouts or slots.

Standing seam The vertical ridge formed where two panels of metal roofing are joined.

Starter course The first course of shingles installed on a roof, starting at the lower edge of the eaves. It is covered by the first course.

Starter strip Mineral-surfaced roll roofing applied at eaves line before application of shingles. Fills spaces of cutouts and joints.

Stepped flashing Flashing along a roof slope against a wall or chimney. Usually consists of L-shaped units that fit into the joint between the roof and the wall.

Storm collar A flashing unit for prefabricated chimney pipe.

Valley The line of intersection of two roof slopes.

Vent An outlet for air (e.g., vent pipe in a plumbing system, ventilating duct).

Vent sleeves or Collars Sheet-metal-flanged collars placed around vent pipes to seal off the roofing around the vent pipe opening.

Weaving or Lacing Interweaving of a course of shingles where there is an intersection in a roof for drainage (e.g., valley).